T0046804

What People Are Saying About James ' Revival Breakthrough...

Many of the predictions of the coming revival ring hollow ____ ____. This is because the predictor seems shallow and Johnny-come-lately. However, James Goll hits us with the certainty and force of a life spent seeking, contending, and verifying his conviction that a global glory is coming. If you read *Revival Breakthrough*, you too will not only believe revival is at the door, but you will also be prepared to embrace it.

—*Mario Murillo*
Evangelist

Revival is coming...are you ready for it? We all long to see true revival come to our nation and the world. What brings revival? Is it all due to a sovereign move of God, or is our participation a necessary ingredient? I say it is both. In his new book, *Revival Breakthrough*, James Goll reveals God's clear pattern of revival and awakening through biblical principles, examples from Scripture and church history, and prophetic words from our own time. Enter into the fires of revival and be part of the next Great Awakening! James clearly shows what you as an individual—and in concert with other believers—can do to prepare your heart and life. Then you can work in partnership with God to bring revival that will lead to widespread awakening and the greatest harvest of souls that the world has ever witnessed!

—*Mike Bickle*
International House of Prayer of Kansas City

James Goll's book *Revival Breakthrough: Preparing for Seasons of Glory, Awakening, and Great Harvest* is indeed a timely message and is, in fact, a true prophetic call to both convict and encourage the body of Christ. As I read this book, the Holy Spirit blew with His sweet wind on the embers of my heart and brought my passionate longing for God's manifest presence to a whole new level. James Goll introduces the reader to profound revelatory insights for this hour, historical accounts of revival, and biblical instruction and positioning for revival. This book built my vision, faith, and expectation for a sovereign move of His Spirit, and I am fully confident it will powerfully influence all who read it.

—*Patricia King*
Minister, author, media producer, and host

James Goll has done it again! This is teaching you can trust and revelation that gets results. The truths presented in *Revival Breakthrough* are the beginning of new breakthroughs for you!

—*Tony Kemp*
Founder, the ACTS Group
President, Tony Kemp Ministries

James Goll's book *Revival Breakthrough* is an excellent and timely overview of the roles of both man and God in fulfilling God's dreams. For decades, James Goll has been in the forefront of many of the movements that have been preparing the way for the next season of God's glory, such as the global prayer movement, personal and national repentance for sin, and the prophetic/apostolic reformation. You will find this book an enlightening, theologically balanced, and passionate guide to the next great awakening. I highly recommend it.

—*Joan Hunter*
Author and evangelist
TV Host, *Miracles Happen!*

Revival is on God's agenda. At this critical moment in time, my dear friend James Goll has released a compelling call for believers to partner with God's breathtaking promises for this generation. With biblical insights and a prophetic edge, *Revival Breakthrough* carries a message that will ignite breakthrough in your life and lead to transformation. I believe we are on the verge of the greatest move of God in history, and this will be the church's finest hour. Take this book to heart and join the movement to spark revival that will last a lifetime!

—*Dr. Ché Ahn*
President, Harvest International Ministry
Senior Pastor, Harvest Rock Church, Pasadena, CA
International Chancellor, Wagner University

In his new book *Revival Breakthrough: Preparing for Seasons of Glory, Awakening, and Great Harvest*, James W. Goll describes a dream that God has—a dream that we can all have a special role in. I want to be a part of His dream, and you will want to be also. This dream is for a great outpouring of God's Spirit to be spread throughout the world with revival and glory! It will be fulfilled as God's people, true believers, fall deeply in love with Him, seeking Him first with complete devotion and pursuing His purposes for their lives. God's glory-dream is that the earth will be filled with people who are reconciled to Him and who intimately know Him—and to whom He can pour out His Spirit and love. This book will provide you with biblical and spiritual guidance for moving forward and seeking the God of the Bible. I especially appreciate the chapter entitled "Revival Manifestations and Phenomena" because I have experienced numerous unusual and extraordinary manifestations over the years. Let's prepare for seasons of glory, awakening, and great harvest throughout the world as we seek *Revival Breakthrough*!

—*Joshua Mills*
Recording artist, keynote conference speaker, and author of more than thirty books, including *Creative Glory*, *Power Portals*, and *Moving in Glory Realms*
www.joshuamills.com

What an exciting time it is right now! The greatest harvest of souls that has ever been known is upon us, and the Lord's glory and presence are flooding the nations! I remember listening to James Goll share with a small group of us about past moves of God—how they grew, what sustained them, and what God birthed out of them— and I felt on fire and excited to be part of this next move. James has always been a forerunner as he hears God's instructions and then plows and lays foundations for us to navigate what is coming next. *Revival Breakthrough* is a guide and a vessel of wisdom for this season we are about to be thrust into. I am so grateful he wrote this book!

—*Ana Werner*
Seer Prophet
Founder and President, Eagles Network
Author, *The Seer's Path*

We all need God's breakthroughs in our lives to fulfill His purposes for us. This is certainly the case with regard to the realm of revival. In his new book *Revival Breakthrough*, James W. Goll writes, "Breakthrough is required for revival because, often, the church has grown dry or cold and is in desperate need of…renewal." God is not content to leave us in that dry state. He wants us to reach out to Him for a new anointing. As James says, "Such a breakthrough begins as we create an opening for God to intervene in our lives and the lives of others." As you read this book, create that opening while you prepare your life for powerful breakthrough in revival and awakening. Then, see what God will do!

—*Matt Sorger*
Prophetic healing revivalist
Author, *God's Unstoppable Breakthrough*
Founder, Glory Life echurch
mattsorger.com

Revival Breakthrough gives voice to the multifaceted study of revival. It will certainly be a foundation that the next generation can learn from to accelerate God's using them to see the end-time harvest of God. James Goll is the real deal. He pulls from wisdom gained through decades of intimacy with God.

—*Cindy Jacobs*
Generals International

James Goll is a father of revival, a pioneer of prayer, and a general in the prophetic. Who better than he to pen in-depth strategies for breakthrough and personally guide us through seasons of glory and awakening? With unparalleled teaching throughout, this book will equip you for the days ahead. *Revival Breakthrough* is a field guide that needs to be in the hands of every believer who is ready for transformation in their own life, family, city, and region.

—*Prophet Charlie Shamp*
Cofounder and President, Destiny Encounters International
Author of five books, including *Mystical Prayer*
www.destinyencounters.com

I have known, received from, and ministered with my friend and spiritual papa, Dr. James Goll, for decades. He has been a voice for the church prophetically, calling her into alignment with the times and seasons of the Lord. In his new book, *Revival Breakthrough*, James reveals God's call for revival and awakening through biblical principles, examples from Scripture and church history, and prophetic words from our own time. Get ready for an adventure into the fires of revival—you get to be part of the next Great Awakening!

—*Steven Springer*
International speaker, author, and friend
President and Cofounder, Global Presence Ministries
Senior Leader, Global Presence Eagles Nest Prophetic School
Apostolic Overseer, Global Presence Apostolic Alliance

We are living in unprecedented times! In the midst of encroaching darkness and a prevailing shaking in the earth, God is ramping up for the greatest season of revival and awakening the world has ever seen. In *Revival Breakthrough*, James Goll sets a course for the church to prepare for history's greatest harvest and manifestation of the glory of God. Come, Lord Jesus, come!

—*Tom and Jane Hamon*
Apostles, Vision Church @ Christian International
Authors of 7 *Anointings for Kingdom Transformation, Dreams and Visions, Discernment,* and *Declarations for Breakthrough*

James Goll has written a prophetic blueprint for an emerging generation of pioneers and reformers. With years of experience and a tender father's heart, he brings us into the plans and purposes of God for this generation. I highly recommend this book to all who are hungry and humble of heart.

—*Jeremiah Johnson*
Founder, The Altar Global
Best-selling author

REVIVAL
BREAKTHROUGH

PREPARING FOR
SEASONS OF GLORY, AWAKENING,
AND GREAT HARVEST

JAMES W. GOLL

WHITAKER
HOUSE

Publisher's Note: This book is not intended to provide medical or psychological advice or to take the place of medical advice and treatment from your personal physician. Those who are having suicidal thoughts or who have been emotionally, physically, or sexually abused should seek help from a mental health professional or qualified counselor. Neither the publisher nor the author nor the author's ministry takes any responsibility for any possible consequences from any action taken by any person reading or following the information in this book. If readers are taking prescription medications, they should consult with their physicians and not take themselves off prescribed medicines without the proper supervision of a physician. Always consult your physician or other qualified health care professional before undertaking any change in your physical regimen, whether fasting, diet, medications, or exercise.

Unless otherwise indicated, all Scripture quotations are taken from the updated *New American Standard Bible*®, © 1960, 1971, 1977, 1995, 2020 by The Lockman Foundation. Used by permission. All rights reserved. (www.Lockman.org). Scripture quotations marked (NIV) are taken from the *Holy Bible, New International Version*®, NIV®, © 1973, 1978, 1984, 2011 by Biblica, Inc.® Used by permission. All rights reserved worldwide. The "NIV" and "New International Version" are trademarks registered in the United States Patent and Trademark Office by Biblica, Inc.® Scripture quotations marked (NKJV) are taken from the *New King James Version*, © 1979, 1980, 1982 by Thomas Nelson, Inc. Used by permission. All rights reserved. Scripture quotations marked (KJV) are taken from the King James Version of the Holy Bible. Scripture quotations marked (NLT) are taken from the *Holy Bible, New Living Translation*, © 1996 by Tyndale House Foundation. Used by permission of Tyndale House Publishers, Inc., Carol Stream, Illinois 60188. All rights reserved. Scripture quotations marked (ESV) are taken from *The Holy Bible, English Standard Version*, © 2000, 2001, 1995 by Crossway Bibles, a division of Good News Publishers. Used by permission. All rights reserved.

Boldface type in the Scripture quotations indicates the author's emphasis.

The forms LORD and GOD (in small capital letters) in Bible quotations represent the Hebrew name for God *Yahweh* (Jehovah), while *Lord* and *God* normally represent the name *Adonai*, in accordance with the Bible version used.

REVIVAL BREAKTHROUGH:
Preparing for Seasons of Glory, Awakening, and Great Harvest

James W. Goll
God Encounters Ministries
P.O. Box 1653 ♦ Franklin, TN 37065
www.godencounters.com ♦ www.GOLLIdeation.com
info@godencounters.com

ISBN: 978-1-64123-840-3♦ eBook ISBN: 978-1-64123-841-0
Printed in the United States of America
© 2022 by James W. Goll

Whitaker House
1030 Hunt Valley Circle ♦ New Kensington, PA 15068
www.whitakerhouse.com

LC record available at https://lccn.loc.gov/2022016202
LC ebook record available at https://lccn.loc.gov/2022016203

No part of this book may be reproduced or transmitted in any form or by any means, electronic or mechanical—including photocopying, recording, or by any information storage and retrieval system—without permission in writing from the publisher. Please direct your inquiries to permissionseditor@whitakerhouse.com.

1 2 3 4 5 6 7 8 9 10 11 ⊔⊔ 29 28 27 26 25 24 23 22

CONTENTS

PART FOUR: THE GREAT HARVEST

FOREWORD

At Global Awakening, the first two statements of our heart for ministry are "For all believers everywhere, we present an opportunity to receive power from God" and "We offer ourselves as evidence that God uses the unqualified when we're willing to take a risk."

James W. Goll wrote *Revival Breakthrough* with the same heart and purpose. I believe this book is going to be a great resource for you. It covers one of my favorite areas of study: revival! True revival is never a human invention. We are not qualified to bring revival or do a work for God on our own. Our role is to participate in what God is doing, but that role involves presenting ourselves to Him in humility and availability, waiting on Him to receive "power from on high."

It is only when we are willing to wait on God—personally and with other believers—that we will see a widespread outpouring of His Spirit. In this book, James describes the process of waiting in humility with prayer and fasting for God's presence and power to manifest in remarkable, transforming, and healing ways. As I often say, "It's not about being the most qualified, most gifted person; if you are willing to take a risk with God, He will use you to awaken others to all that Jesus is." *Revival Breakthrough* includes striking illustrations of people who were willing to take that risk.

They drew close to God and became His instruments to reach others with the message of His grace and salvation, and they saw the power of God's Spirit save multitudes and change society. This book is an invitation for you to take the same risk for the sake of the gospel.

I have known James for thirty-six years, and, throughout all those years, I have seen his passion for God and for revival. He has authored many books on the subjects of prayer, prophecy, the gifts of the Spirit, and the moving of the Spirit. *Revival Breakthrough* is not written from the mind of an armchair academic but from the heart of a prophet who loves revival and also has personal experience with and relevant knowledge of the topic. James writes with passion, deep insight, and biblical knowledge. If you love revival, you will want this book for your library because its message is a "now" message!

Blessings in and through Him,

Randy Clark, D.D., D.Min., Th.D., M.Div., B.S. Religious Studies
Overseer, Apostolic Network of Global Awakening
President, Global Awakening Theological Seminary

PREFACE: GOD HAS A DREAM

"Arise, shine; for your light has come,
and the glory of the LORD has risen upon you."
—Isaiah 60:1

I walk in the spiritual gift of prophecy, and I receive many dreams from God while on assignments for Him. I have dreams about people and subjects that are important to the Lord. Recently, as I was going to sleep, I prayed, "God, do *You* have a dream? If You have a dream, would You like to share Your dream with me? And if You share Your dream with me, would You give me permission to share Your dream with others?"

After this, I fell asleep and had a very simple dream in which I saw myself sitting up in bed with my Bible open. In this dream, I could hear myself reading from Isaiah 60:1–3:

> *Arise, shine; for your light has come, and the glory of the LORD has risen upon you. For behold, darkness will cover the earth and deep darkness the peoples; but the LORD will arise upon you and His glory will appear upon you. Nations will come to your light, and kings to the brightness of your rising.*

I awoke from this dream to find myself sitting up in bed with my arms out as if they were holding something. I was also prophesying from both the above portion of Scripture and Habakkuk 2:14, saying, "Arise, shine, for the glory of the Lord is risen upon you. And the knowledge of the glory of the Lord is going to cover the earth as the waters cover the seas."

I have a prophetic word for you: God has a dream in His heart, and it is about a *great harvest of souls* for His kingdom. It is about God's people being *transformed* more and more into the image of His Son Jesus. Most of all, it is about the manifestation of *His glory*. Part of God's dream is for His glory to come to the world anew and increasingly spread throughout the earth. We are entering into a movement of the Holy Spirit that is a "latter glory of God" dream. Haggai 2:9 says, "'The glory of this present house will be greater than the glory of the former house,' says the LORD Almighty. 'And in this place I will grant peace,' declares the LORD Almighty" (NIV).

God wants to share this dream with us. He welcomes us to partner with Him to fulfill His purposes. The great harvest will come when God's people have a breakthrough of revival—a movement of the Holy Spirit in our midst in which we are cleansed, empowered, healed, and commissioned so we can truly be partners with Him. This movement will transform not only us but also the world around us as multitudes of people see and experience the great, latter-day glory of God.

In *Revival Breakthrough: Preparing for Seasons of Glory, Awakening, and Great Harvest*, I invite you to come on this revival journey with me in a very personal manner. I really want you to engage with me from your heart. I hope you will enter into this journey for the sake of your family, your neighborhood, your city, and your nation.

From the very beginning of this book, I want you to know how much I depend on God and His Spirit to touch your heart through His wisdom that I share in these pages. Otherwise, all you will read is a collection of really well-formatted information—biblically sound and historically accurate but with no impact. It takes hearts engaged with the Almighty for breakthrough to occur.

Revival Breakthrough begins with seasoned lessons made new to us today. We will look at many portions of Scripture as we explore the foundational importance of prayer for revival and the vital aspect of fasting, including how sacrifice releases God's presence and power. We will review exciting occurrences of revival and their characteristics through the ages, and we will note the four stages of revival, awakening, reformation, and transformation. We will culminate with contemporary prophetic promises of the coming great harvest.

Let's pray together that we may fully respond to God's dream. May our hearts agree together for *Revival Breakthrough* as we prepare for a great, unprecedented harvest that will fill the world with His glory!

Father, we submit ourselves to You. We are so grateful to be alive in this hour, grateful that we get to be Annas and Simeons, or a younger generation of Your servants, who can be part of what has been promised for decades and generations. We are a chosen people, we are a royal priesthood, and we are ministers unto You. We are chosen for such a time as this. God our Father, we magnify and exalt You and the Lord Jesus Christ. We love the Holy Spirit and His presence with us. We ask for Your grace and power to fulfill all that You have called us to do in partnership with You to bring Your dream to reality. In Jesus's name, Amen!

PART ONE:

PRAYER OPENS THE HEAVENS

1

CREATING AN OPENING

*"When Jesus came back to Capernaum a few days later, it was heard
that He was at home. And many were gathered together, so that there
was no longer space, not even near the door; and He was speaking the
word to them. And some people came, bringing to Him a man who
was paralyzed, carried by four men. And when they were unable to
get to Him because of the crowd, they removed the roof above Him;
and after **digging an opening**, they let down the pallet on which the
paralyzed man was lying. And Jesus, seeing their faith,
said to the paralyzed man, 'Son, your sins are forgiven.'"*
—Mark 2:1–5

What is *revival?*

And why do we need *breakthrough* to experience it?

"Revival" may be defined in a variety of ways, and we will explore
the meanings and characteristics of revival throughout the coming chapters. Essentially, revival is a season of powerful visitation from God that
includes the presence of the Holy Spirit made manifest: the God of heaven
is felt and recognized in a tangible way on earth.

When the Lord shows up in this way, His church is restored to life,
and believers have a renewed love for the Lord Jesus Christ. God's people

become true salt and light, demonstrating His love and power to a spiritually needy world, serving as carriers of His glory throughout the earth.

Breakthrough is required for revival because, often, the church has grown dry or cold and is in desperate need of the renewal I described above. Such a breakthrough begins as we create an opening for God to intervene in our lives and the lives of others.

In each chapter of this book, we will look at a theme verse or passage from Scripture that helps us to focus on God's dream of revival among His people, a great harvest of souls, and a world filled with His glory. Our theme Scripture for this first chapter of *Revival Breakthrough* is a gospel lesson, but I will be unwrapping it for us in the manner of a parable.

As we will do at the start of every chapter in order to prepare our hearts to be touched by God's Spirit for revival, let's begin with prayer:

Father, thank You so much for the Word of God and for the example of our Lord Jesus Christ. We ask You to illuminate for us this entire event from the second chapter of Mark that took place at Jesus's home in Capernaum, as well as the parable it becomes for us. Holy Spirit, please take us into these words, into this event, and help us to see things we've never seen before about creating open heavens on behalf of others. We are grateful that You are more than willing and able to reveal Yourself to us through Your Word—even to the point of blowing the roofs off our spiritual houses to make Jesus not only a welcome Guest in our lives but also our Homeowner. Amen!

JESUS AT HOME WITH US

To unfold the meaning of our theme passage, let's examine the above five verses from Mark 2 one at a time so we can glean as much insight into the event as possible.

YEARNING FOR GOD'S "HOUSE"

When Jesus came back to Capernaum a few days later, it was heard that He was at home.   (Mark 2:1)

Jesus was at home. Don't you just love that phrase? And isn't that what our goal is to be—for Jesus to feel at home in our lives? Yes! Is Jesus at home in your house, your family, your congregation, your city? He said, *"Anyone who loves me will obey my teaching. My Father will love them, and we will come to them and make our home with them"* (John 14:23 NIV).

I believe many churches and individual believers have set the bar too low when it comes to experiencing the manifest presence of God—or whatever phraseology you prefer to use to describe when the Lord "shows up" in glory and power. Unfortunately, for many believers, when He does show up, it's more of an exception than a regular occurrence in which they joyfully exclaim, "Wow, it's God again!" I think that's an unnatural state of affairs for God's sons and daughters. Too often, we treat Him like He's only a Guest in our home rather than the Homeowner that He truly is. What might you need to do to have Him be more than just an honored Guest who occasionally shows up in your life?

Note also that as children of God the Father, we are invited to His house—*His* house. For too long, many believers and their leaders have made church and ministry all about themselves. At those times when Jesus manifests His presence, most people don't know what to do or even how to acknowledge Him. It's no wonder He doesn't tend to show up very often. Do you like showing up at homes where you don't feel welcome? Nope, neither do I.

Not long ago, I was inside my house, and I went to open the front door. No one had knocked on the door or rung the doorbell, but I intentionally opened the door as a prayerful act of inviting Jesus to come into my home. Have you actively, physically, verbally, and prayerfully invited Jesus into your house? Have you invited Jesus into your kitchen, your living room, your dining room, your bedroom? I have invited Jesus to come into every room in my house. If you haven't done the same, I encourage you to do so today. Welcome Him to come and stay as your Homeowner.

HUNGRY FOR REVELATION

And many were gathered together, so that there was no longer space, not even near the door; and He was speaking the word to them.

(Mark 2:2)

When Jesus is in His "temple," feeling at home, people gather, and revelation rests on the Word of God. In this particular event, God's house overflowed with crowds to such an extent that people could not find a place to sit; they congregated around the doors and around the windows outside to hear what Jesus was saying. There are other places in the Gospels that speak of similar gatherings. The people in attendance at such meetings hung on His every word. I need to return to that kind of hunger, to that point of wanting to—needing to—hang on Jesus's every word, to every word I read in the Bible. How about you?

DESPERATE FOR CHANGE

And some people came, bringing to Him a man who was paralyzed, carried by four men. (Mark 2:3)

Four men became desperate for a physical breakthrough for their friend who was paralyzed. They carried the man, perhaps a great distance, to see the Healer. Their compassion led them to sacrifice their time and effort to give their friend hope—putting faith to work.

What are you desperate for? What stirs your compassion? Are you putting your faith to work in that situation?

DETERMINED TO SEE GOD WORK

And when they were unable to get to Him because of the crowd, they removed the roof above Him; and after digging an opening, they let down the pallet on which the paralyzed man was lying. (Mark 2:4)

The five men must have been disappointed and frustrated when they first arrived and realized they could not get close to Jesus. The four who had been carrying their friend were probably also hot, sweaty, tired, thirsty, and hungry. Seeing the crowd, they could have given up in discouragement. I understand such a feeling. Sometimes, I am really tempted to give up during my journey of believing for the great harvest. But they didn't, and I don't either.

Although weary from their journey, and seeing the obstacles before them, the men moved from the natural to the supernatural to find the solution they needed: "We'll tear the roof off the house!" While the meeting was going on, the men went up to the roof to break open a portion of it, probably with their bare hands. I can imagine the dust and dirt flying through the air and sifting down to the ground as they dug the opening. With great effort and determination, they made progress toward creating the hole. It was like opening up the heavens.

Of course, they couldn't just drop their friend down through a small hole; they had to make quite a large opening, maybe about six feet long and four feet wide, to accommodate both the stretcher and the ropes. No doubt, their digging caused some commotion among the people gathered below. Then they lowered their friend in front of Jesus. This was an actual *physical* revival breakthrough! Even though it meant disrupting the whole meeting, the men were determined to bring their friend into the presence of the living Messiah.

How much determination do you have to bring your friends and loved ones into the presence of Jesus for healing or deliverance?

FULL OF FAITH FOR BREAKTHROUGH

And Jesus, seeing their faith, said to the paralyzed man, "Son, your sins are forgiven."   (Mark 2:5)

This verse *doesn't* say that Jesus saw the faith of the paralytic. Neither does it say that Jesus *didn't* see faith of the paralytic. It says that Jesus saw "*their faith.*" Sometimes, that's all it takes. Not *one* person's faith but our *combined* faith. Jesus saw *all their faith together.*

Then Jesus spoke to the paralytic. But He didn't say, "Arise and be healed." (How dare You, Jesus, after all their efforts!) Instead, He spoke a deeper word, a revival breakthrough word. He spoke to the man's heart and soul. Jesus saw *their* faith, and now He spoke to the paralytic man, saying, "*Son, your sins are forgiven*"—and the man's body was healed at the same time. May these words echo through our lives today and heal the sick body of Christ to be raised to wholeness.

Now that's a parable for us to ingest and digest!

OPEN HEAVENS

I have written extensively about "open heavens" in my book *The Seer*.[1] I am gratified that many people consider this book to be the standard on the topic and a contemporary classic. When speaking about open heavens, I always turn to three specific Scripture passages: Genesis 28:12–17, Matthew 3:16–17, and Mark 2:1–5, which we just examined. Let's now look at the other two passages.

> And [Jacob] had a dream, and behold, a ladder was set up on the earth with its top reaching to heaven; and behold, the angels of God were ascending and descending on it. Then behold, the LORD was standing above it and said, "I am the LORD, the God of your father Abraham and the God of Isaac; the land on which you lie I will give to you and to your descendants. Your descendants will also be like the dust of the earth, and you will spread out to the west and to the east, and to the north and to the south; and in you and in your descendants shall all the families of the earth be blessed. Behold, I am with you and will keep you wherever you go, and will bring you back to this land; for I will not leave you until I have done what I have promised you." Then Jacob awoke from his sleep and said, "The LORD is certainly in this place, and I did not know it!" And he was afraid and said, "How awesome is this place! This is none other than the house of God, and this is the gate of heaven!" (Genesis 28:12–17)

As Jacob experienced in his life, we need the gate of heaven to open over our lives, families, churches, cities, and nations.

> After He was baptized, Jesus came up immediately from the water; and behold, the heavens were opened, and he saw the Spirit of God descending as a dove and settling on Him, and behold, a voice from the heavens said, "This is My beloved Son, with whom I am well pleased." (Matthew 3:16–17)

The heavens were opened over Jesus when He was baptized in water by John the Baptist. The voice of the Father came from the heavens, acknowledging how pleased He was with His Son.

---

1. James W. Goll, *The Seer* (Shippensburg, PA: Destiny Image Publishers, 2012).

One time, the Holy Spirit inwardly spoke to me, asking, "What does My Word say happens when an open heaven occurs?" I did a quick Holy Spirit Bible study as I anticipated His answer. I realized that one of the things that happens when an open heaven occurs is that the Father speaks. It happened in Matthew 3, and it also occurred in Genesis 28. In Jacob's dream, God stood at the top of the ladder and spoke to the patriarch, saying, *"In you and in your descendants shall all the families of the earth be blessed."* At Jesus's baptism, the Father spoke from heaven and said, *"This is My beloved Son, with whom I am well pleased."* What happened in that event? *The Father spoke His approval.* His blessings are released in an open heaven.

As in Mark 2:1–5, we need to "blow the roof off" of our limited mindsets and thinking so we can believe the Lord for extraordinary works of grace in our world. Desperate times require desperate measures. We need desperate laborers to arise—those who are not content with the status quo but are willing to expend themselves in order to lower other people into the presence of the same dear Lord Jesus Christ.

THREE KEYS TO OPEN HEAVENS, MINDS, AND DOORS

At least three keys are needed to open heavens, minds, and doors for revival breakthrough: (1) *prayer and fasting*, (2) *God's presence*, and (3) *prophetic revelation*. I believe each of these aspects can be demonstrated biblically and historically with regard to the elements that precede revival. Let's briefly look at all three elements, which we will explore in greater detail as we progress through this book.

KEY #1: PRAYER AND FASTING

Prayer with fasting is a powerful key to making an opening for breakthrough. One of my favorite revival testimonies comes from the 1949–52 Hebrides Revival. The Hebrides is a set of islands off the northwest coast of Scotland. Two sisters, Peggy and Christine Smith, eighty-four and eighty-two years old, respectively, were desperate for revival on Isle of Lewis, where they lived. They had actually experienced historic revival previously, so they knew how to pray according to the Scriptures. They reminded God of His word from Isaiah 44:3: *"For I will pour water on the thirsty land and streams on the dry ground; I will pour out My Spirit on your offspring, and My blessing on your descendants."*

Every day, Peggy and Christine prayed the promises of God for the residents of their village of Barvas. They interceded for an open heaven and revival. As they prayed the Word, they began to claim another open-heaven verse, Isaiah 64:1: *"Oh, that You would tear open the heavens and come down, that the mountains would quake at Your presence."*

One morning, Peggy, who was blind, received a vision from God of "the churches crowded with people, including many young people, and hundreds being swept into the kingdom. She saw the Lamb in the midst of the throne with the keys of heaven in his hand (Rev. 5:6; Matt. 16:18)."[2] That evening, the Spirit of God fell on seven young men gathered in a barn who had asked God to purify their lives and who had been praying for months from Isaiah 62:6–7, which says, *"On your walls, Jerusalem, I have appointed watchmen; all day and all night they will never keep silent. You who profess the LORD, take no rest for yourselves; and give Him no rest until He establishes and makes Jerusalem an object of praise on the earth."*

So, while Peggy and Christine were praying, and Peggy had a visitation, and while a little band of young men was in a barn offering prayers according to Isaiah 62, the Spirit fell on those young men. Sure enough, God came. It was the joining of generations to such an extent that Peggy "sent word to Rev. MacKay [her pastor] that God had shown her He was going to send a mighty revival. She asked him to call together the elders and deacons of the church for special times of waiting on God for revival." Rev. MacKay sought someone who could lead revival meetings. Soon, evangelist Duncan Campbell was called to come help with the revival.[3] Campbell would stay for three years.[4]

This ingredient of revival—a prayerful desperation to see God move in our midst—is always within me, and it can be within you too. Our hearts are God's altar, and, like the fire for the burnt offering at the tabernacle, His fire is supposed to be kept continually burning on the altar; it should never go out. (See Leviticus 6:8–13.) Those two elderly women

2. Wesley Duewel, *Revival Fire* (Grand Rapids, MI: Zondervan, 1995), chap. 40, Kindle.
3. Duewel, *Revival Fire*, chap. 40.
4. Duncan Campbell, "The Revival on the Isle of Lewis," SermonIndex.net, audio recording.

on the Isle of Lewis knew God's Word and prayed God's Word; likewise, we should know and pray the Word. That group of young men in the barn knew the Word and prayed the Word, and all who gathered there were blessed beyond measure. The Holy Spirit fell on them personally and on the Hebrides Islands as well.

Duncan Campbell is known as the revival breakthrough pastor of the Hebrides Revival. However, he emphatically stated that he took no personal credit for the revival, insisting that it was fully a work of God in which he was merely grateful to participate, saying, "I don't carry revival about with me in my pocket. Revival broke out in Lewis some time before I went to the island. I thank God for the privilege of being in its midst for over three years.… And I am thankful to God for the privilege of, perhaps in some small way, leading that movement and teaching the young converts in the deep things of God."[5]

It is said that, in the Hebrides Islands Revival, a type of "spiritual radiation zone" was created. When people walked into that zone, they would come under experiential conviction of sin, and many souls were saved. *That* is revival breakthrough—and it was preceded by prayer.

To understand more about the power of prayer for revival, let's look next at the testimony of Evan Roberts and the great Welsh Revival of 1904–05. That revival was different from the Hebrides Revival, yet, in some respects, it was quite similar. At the age of thirteen, Evan Roberts began to seek the Lord,[6] and when he was twenty-six, revival came to his hometown. He taught the people to pray two simple prayers: (1) "Send the Spirit now, for Jesus Christ's sake";[7] and (2) "Send the Spirit now more powerfully for Jesus Christ's sake."[8] Indeed, God's Spirit came down, and more than a hundred thousand souls were swept up into God's kingdom.[9]

As a teenager, Roberts worked in the coal mines. He asked an elder in the church, "When God first comes, where does God come?" The elder replied, "Well, when God first shows up, He shows up at a prayer meeting." Roberts said, "I want to be where God's going to be," so he started

---

5. Campbell, "The Revival on the Isle of Lewis."
6. Duewel, *Revival Fire*, chap. 23.
7. Duewel, chap. 25.
8. Duewel, chap. 25.
9. Duewel, chaps. 24 and 25.

attending prayer meetings. No matter the church or denomination, if there was a prayer meeting, he was present.

Roberts briefly moved to the northern part of Wales to attend Bible college. While he was there, Seth Joshua, a minister and evangelist, spoke at a meeting that Roberts attended. Joshua released a prayer that went out in the Spirit and, like an arrow, struck Evan Roberts. Roberts came under conviction and returned to his hometown particularly to seek the salvation of his siblings. Roberts's continual, intense prayers and seeking of God helped to pave the way for a powerful outbreak of revival in Wales.

How do I know these things? I enjoy reading testimonies and biographies of revivalists and others who have greatly impacted people for the advancement of God's kingdom.[10] I've been to Moriah Chapel, known throughout the globe as the birthplace of the Welsh Revival. I have traveled the world re-digging the spiritual wells that were dug before me, and I have earnestly prayed for revival.

In the church today, this cry is rising: "More, Lord!" There must be a spiritual revolution among the youth as there was with Evan Roberts in Wales and the young men gathered in the barn on the Isle of Lewis. We must have a *transgenerational* anointing. It's time for prayer to arise that will blow the roofs off houses worldwide with God's glory.

KEY #2: GOD'S PRESENCE

The one outstanding and distinguishing characteristic of God's people is His presence among us. After Moses asked God, *"Please, show me Your glory!"* (Exodus 33:18), God revealed His glorious presence to him. Just as Moses did, let us ask God for a manifestation of His presence:

> *Then* [Moses] *said to* [the Lord], *"If Your presence does not go with us, do not lead us up from here."… The* LORD *said to Moses, "I will also do this thing of which you have spoken; for you have found favor in My sight and I have known you by name." Then Moses said, "Please,*

10. I highly recommend the following resources on revival: Duncan Campbell, *Fire on the Altar* (Destiny Image, 2000), audio cassette; Wesley Duewel, *Revival Fire* (Grand Rapids, MI: Zondervan, 1995); Winkie Pratney, *Revival: Principles to Change the World* (Lindale, TX: Ministry of Helps, 2010); Leonard Ravenhill, *Why Revival Tarries* (Minneapolis, MN: Bethany House, 2004); and Robert Backhouse, ed., *The Classics of Revival* (London: Hodder & Stoughton, 1996).

show me Your glory!" And He said, "I Myself will make all My good-
ness pass before you, and will proclaim the name of the LORD before
you; and I will be gracious to whom I will be gracious, and will show
compassion to whom I will show compassion."

(Exodus 33:15, 17–19)

In the tabernacle, the bread of God's presence, also called the "show-
bread," was used by the priest in ministering to the Lord. *"And you shall set*
the bread of the Presence on the table before Me continually" (Exodus 25:30).
Jesus is the Bread of Life, and we are to partake of His life daily if we want
the presence of God continually in our midst.

We need the presence of God more than anything in this life. Let me
share a significant event I experienced that enabled me to better understand how we are to invite His presence. In January 1999, while I was
having a special time of rest, the Lord visited me in a remarkable, piercing
dream that gripped my soul and helped to set the course of my life from
that day forward. I believe that the message of this dream is still a very clear
word to all God's people today.

In the dream, I was holding three long loaves of bread, each wrapped
in its own little napkin at one end. I was holding these loaves of bread close
to my chest, right over my heart. I then reached for my daughter Rachel's
aqua baby blanket, which she'd had since birth. She loved that blanket.
It was warm and fuzzy, and she carried it with her everywhere. My wife,
Michal Ann, and I allowed Rachel, our youngest daughter, to carry this
"security blanket"; even though she was no longer a baby, seeing her toting
it around was very endearing to us. Through this symbol, the Lord was
communicating to me in a way He knew would enable me to best understand His message.

In the dream, I wrapped the three loaves of bread in this special blanket. The napkin around the bottom portion of each loaf was similar to a
diaper. I was holding the bundle of loaves over my heart, cuddling it, and
rocking gently side to side, as a parent does with a newborn child.

Then I heard the words, "When My people will care for, cherish, nurture, and love the bread of My presence like a parent does their newborn
child, then revival will come." I repeated these words.

Following this, I awakened from the dream. My arms were positioned as if I was holding or cradling something, and I was rocking gently. The manifest presence of God was there with me in my bedroom. Then I heard myself prophesying what I had just heard myself prophesy in the dream. I was repeating, "When My people will care for, cherish, nurture, and love the bread of My presence like a parent does their newborn child, then revival will come."

As I heard myself repeat those words, just as I had done in the dream, the sweet presence of the Holy Spirit lingered, saturating my whole being. The Lord was emphasizing these words by having me repeat them twice and possibly three times. This I know: He wants us to cherish and care for His presence, pray for His presence, love His presence, and nurture His presence. After all, isn't that what we have longed for all our lives? Isn't that what we were created for—to be carriers of His most brilliant presence? Isn't this the answer to what the church is really crying out for?

Revival will come when we get up in the middle of the night for the night feedings and hold the "child of new beginnings" close to our heart and wash this child with love and compassion. I pray, "Let the cry arise, and let His presence come forth!" We must pray earnestly, in full submission to God's purposes, as Jesus did:

> *During the days of Jesus' life on earth, he offered up prayers and petitions with fervent cries and tears to the one who could save him from death, and he was heard because of his reverent submission.*
>
> (Hebrews 5:7 NIV)

KEY #3: PROPHETIC REVELATION

The prophetic dimension is a powerful tool to open closed minds, closed doors, and closed situations to the reality and power of God. Seek the Lord through reading His Word, and you will receive this key. Then, insert the key into the keyhole, turn it, and open wide the door. The following Scriptures will help us to understand this aspect of revival breakthrough.

> *Man shall not live on bread alone, but man shall live on everything that comes out of the mouth of the LORD.* (Deuteronomy 8:3)

In Matthew 4:4, Jesus spoke the same words: *"But He answered and said, 'It is written: "Man shall not live on bread alone, but on every word that comes out of the mouth of God."'"* We need to live on the ever-proceeding Word of God. We can live abundantly and purposefully only as we receive what God has already said to us in His Word and what He is saying to us particularly today through prophecy, words of wisdom, words of knowledge, and other spiritual gifts.

> *And take the helmet of salvation and the sword of the Spirit, which is the word of God.* (Ephesians 6:17)

The *"two-edged sword"* of the Spirit (see Hebrews 4:12) is the Word of God. We must use this key to open the door to God's presence and not prevent others from entering in, as was the custom of some religious gatekeepers during the time of Jesus. Jesus said, *"But woe to you, scribes and Pharisees, hypocrites, because you shut the kingdom of heaven in front of people; for you do not enter it yourselves, nor do you allow those who are entering to go in"* (Matthew 23:13). The scribes and Pharisees had the keys, but they used them only so they themselves could enter, while they hindered others. Instead, in the name of Jesus, let us use the keys of revelation to enter in and open the doors wide so that many others may enter in also.

STEPS TO VISITATION

Bringing this all together, let us now consider steps to experiencing a visitation from God by looking at a "Pool of Bethesda parable" based on this significant passage from John's gospel:

> *Now in Jerusalem, by the Sheep Gate, there is a pool which in Hebrew is called Bethesda, having five porticoes. In these porticoes lay a multitude of those who were sick, blind, limping, or paralyzed. Now a man was there who had been ill for thirty-eight years. Jesus, upon seeing this man lying there and knowing that he had already been in that condition for a long time, said to him, "Do you want to get well?" The sick man answered Him, "Sir, I have no man to put me into the pool when the water is stirred up, but while I am coming, another steps down before me." Jesus said to him, "Get up, pick up your pallet and walk."*

> *Immediately the man became well, and picked up his pallet and began*
> *to walk. Now it was a Sabbath on that day.*   (John 5:2–9)

Jesus personally visited an infirm man who was lying by the Pool of Bethesda and asked him what seems to be an obvious question: *"Do you want to get well?"* The man didn't immediately say yes; rather, he answered out of disappointment, *"Sir, I have no man to put me into the pool when the water is stirred up, but while I am coming, another steps down before me."* The man explained why he thought he couldn't be healed, not fully accepting the fact that Jesus, the Healer, was visiting him. The very One who had come down from heaven to bring wholeness to all who would believe was standing before him.

Often, when individuals have been sick for a long period of time, they become identified with their illnesses. Other people see them primarily in light of their sicknesses, and sometimes even those who are ill see themselves as their maladies or as perpetually in that infirm condition with no hope of recovery.

That was this man's mindset. However, just as he experienced, we can encounter the One who came to give us life and wholeness. We can see demonstrations of His glory in revivals and great harvests. A visitation from the Lord, or from one of the Lord's angels on His mission, encompasses four steps:

1. Waiting (in this case, the man was waiting for the water to stir)

2. Expecting (anticipating the visitation)

3. Accepting the Holy Spirit's presence already with us (in our hearts and spirits)

4. Knowing that God can and will visit us again and again; all we have to do is ask

When we wait, expect, and accept—and when we know that the Lord will visit us—our prayer must be that His presence would be released in the greatest measure in the pool of our hearts and spirits. We pray this so that He will bring forth mighty visitations that will fulfill His purposes in us and bring Him the greatest glory.

The man at the Pool of Bethesda said there was no one to help him get into the pool. Again, he was unaware of the identity of the Man who stood before him, ready and more than able to heal him by the living water that flowed within Him. We know that the Man is Jesus. The Son of God has already come, and sometimes we miss the day of His visitation because we don't recognize He is already with us. Our great gifted One has come and now lives within every believer.

There's much more to glean from this passage of Scripture, but those are a few steps to visitation for us to consider along our journey toward revival breakthrough. Will you create an opening for God to move in your life by following these steps to visitation and by activating the keys of prayer and fasting, God's presence, and prophetic revelation?

LET'S PRAY TOGETHER

Father God, we want Jesus to be at home in our lives, and we believe that authentic revival can start in us—right here, right now. We open the door of our hearts. Jesus, please come in and be our Homeowner, Restorer, and Lord. Our hearts are no longer our homes; they are Yours. As we yearn for revival, we look to precedents in Scripture and in human history, such as the Hebrides Revival, the Welsh Revival, and many other outpourings of Your Spirit. We lift our cry to You: what You did before, we pray, "Do it again!" We want to partner with the Holy Spirit to create open heavens for our lives, our families, our churches, our cities, and our nations. We desire to be a people of Your presence. We want to love, cherish, and care for the bread of Your presence, just as loving parents care for their newborn child. We wait for You, we expect You, we accept Your indwelling presence, and we know that You can and will visit us again…and again. Amen!

2

WHEN GOD LISTENS TO THE VOICE OF MAN

"All these were continually devoting themselves with one mind to prayer, along with the women, and Mary the mother of Jesus, and with His brothers."
—Acts 1:14

You may consider the title of this chapter unusual, thinking, "James, doesn't God always listen to people's prayers?" Well, in revival history, there are those very special, strategic, kairos times when you know that you know that you know that God has turned His head earthward and heard the prayers of an individual who "stood in the gap." This phrase comes from Ezekiel 22:30: *"I searched for a man among them who would build up a wall and stand in the gap before Me for the land, so that I would not destroy it; but I found no one."* God is still searching for people who will stand in the gap, people who will come together in unity with others for the purpose of crucial intercessory prayer.

Our theme Scripture for this chapter is Acts 1:14: *"All these were continually devoting themselves with one mind to prayer, along with the women, and Mary the mother of Jesus, and with His brothers."* These praying people, a group of about a hundred and twenty people (see verse 15), surely had God's ear because they loved His Son, Jesus, and were all interceding as one.

As we begin to unfold more principles for intercession, let's pray together with the same unity of heart and mind to see God work among us.

Father, we desire to be faithful intercessors who stand in the gap for our families, communities, and nations. As the united people of God, we agree together in harmony of heart and mind, asking that You would use us to pray in this way. Let Your purposes be manifest on earth as they are in heaven! May multitudes be delivered from sin, sickness, destruction, and death as they experience the power and joy of Your kingdom. In Jesus's name, Amen and Amen.

EIGHT QUALITIES OF GODLY INTERCESSORS

What does it mean to be devoted to prayer like the early believers were? Such singular and amazing revival intercessors share characteristics that we need to take to heart and emulate.[11] Here are eight qualities that revival intercessors have in common:

1. They love and trust God supremely above all.

2. They have a deep heart response to the urgent need of the moment. This is the "prophetic intercessor" side of their prayers.

3. They are self-sacrificing and ready to give their all to God. Revival intercessors are true disciples.

4. They often sense the need for a genuine, very personal, and corporate response with repentance. (We will unwrap this point in a forthcoming chapter on repentance.)

5. They identify with the sins and needs—take careful note of this— of an entire generation, of an entire nation or people group, or to address a specific injustice, such as abortion, rights for the first nations and indigenous peoples, and so forth.

6. They exhibit thorough, contrite, humble prayer that often includes the sacrifice of fasting.

---

11. For more in-depth studies on aspects of prayer, visit www.godencounters.com and click on my online prayer classes entitled "Hearing God's Voice Today," "Powerful Prophetic Intercession," "Tending the Fires of Intercession," "Prayers That Strike the Mark," and others.

7. They often are those who rally other believers to participate because they know that this type of prayer is better engaged in jointly. When revival intercessors get ahold of you, they immediately want to activate you into their prayer life, assuring you, "We're going to wrestle this thing together! God will hear us."

8. They have a determined, strong expectation that God will answer their earnest pleas. This is what it means to seek revival breakthrough—to prepare earnestly for the great harvest.

Revival intercessors call people together as a group as if they have a supernatural trumpet. They often invite others to this task of miraculous intervention by requesting prayers for protection, provision, deliverance, and transformation.

Such intercessors can't be shaken loose from their purpose of moving God's heart. They're like a tenacious bulldog tightly biting someone's pant leg. I have a mini Goldendoodle named Destiny that thinks she's a circus dog. When someone, anyone, comes to visit, she jumps and jumps and jumps. Of course, I command, "Down, Destiny. Sit. Stay." But no, Destiny continues to jump—there's no stopping her until she receives the attention she demands. Similarly, revival intercessors are dogged in their prayers, and we should be too.

MOSES'S TENACIOUS PRAYERS

To help us understand what moves the heart of God to listen to the voice of man, let's look at two passages from the life of Moses found in the books of Exodus and Numbers. Known for his tenacious prayers, Moses made holy arguments before God on behalf of others that prevailed and released God to act. As we review these Scriptures, note that *mercy* is the key theme.

A CRISIS OF DISOBEDIENCE

The first passage is from Exodus 32, beginning with verse 9:[12]

---

12. In my book *The Mystery of Israel and the Middle East, A Prophetic Gaze into the Future* (Ada, MI: Chosen Books, 2021), I do a deep dive into Exodus 32 and other Scriptures. Here, I am highlighting the most important aspects relating to revival breakthrough.

Then the LORD said to Moses, "I have seen this people, and behold, they are an obstinate people."

God has no problem saying what He means! The context of this verse is the Israelites' rebellion in making a golden calf to worship as their god while Moses was on Mount Sinai worshipping the true God and receiving the Ten Commandments. The Lord continued,

So now leave Me alone, that My anger may burn against them and that I may destroy them; and I will make of you a great nation.
(Exodus 32:10)

That's pretty intense language. I don't think that God has bad days and good days, like we do. However, from a human perspective, if He were to have any bad days, this would seem to be one of them. It's as if God is saying, "I'm going to start all over, Moses. Forget those guys; they're just stubborn and obstinate. It's just you and Me, and we're going to build a new and great nation."

APPEALING TO GOD'S REDEEMING WORKS AND REPUTATION

When Moses heard this, what was his response?

Then Moses pleaded with the LORD his God, and said, "LORD, why does Your anger burn against Your people whom You have brought out from the land of Egypt with great power and with a mighty hand? Why should the Egyptians talk, saying, 'With evil motives He brought them out, to kill them on the mountains and to destroy them from the face of the earth'? Turn from Your burning anger and relent of doing harm to Your people."   (Exodus 32:11–12)

Moses was presenting an argument to God on behalf of the people. He was essentially expressing, "God, You don't really want to start all over. I agree that the people are obstinate, but, by the way, so am I, and I'm their leader. So, why would You want to start over with me?" Then Moses made an appeal, saying, in effect, "If You start all over, what is the world going to say? What are the Egyptians going to think if You blot out Your own people? They will believe that You brought the Israelites out of Egypt solely for the purpose of annihilating them from the face of the earth. I ask You to turn from Your burning anger and change Your mind about them."

APPEALING TO GOD'S FAITHFULNESS AND PROMISE

Then Moses asked God to remember His promise to His people:

Remember Abraham, Isaac, and Israel [Jacob], Your servants to whom You swore by Yourself, and said to them, "I will multiply your descendants as the stars of the heavens, and all this land of which I have spoken I will give to your descendants, and they shall inherit it forever." (Exodus 32:13)

After Moses pleaded with the Lord, God changed His mind about destroying the Israelites:

So the LORD relented of the harm which He said He would do to His people. (Exodus 32:14)

Wait, what just happened here? It is a biblical principle that God does not change. For example, Malachi 3:6 says, *"For I, the LORD, do not change; therefore you, the sons of Jacob, have not come to an end."* These two Scriptures would seem to be in conflict.

Not if we dig deeper. To summarize:

- ✦ Moses's argument was based on the history of God's redeeming works for Israel. He told the Lord that it would be out of His character with His great acts of mercy if He destroyed Israel now. (See Exodus 32:11.)

- ✦ Next, Moses argued on the basis of the glory of God's name, saying, in essence, "Do not give the Egyptians a reason to slander You, claiming that You do not provide and care for Your own people." (See verse 12.)

- ✦ Finally, Moses argued according to God's faithfulness to His loyal servants, Abraham, Isaac, and Jacob, and the promise that He had previously given to them. Moses boldly quoted this promise to God and held Him accountable to His own word. (See verse 13.)

So, did God change? We must remember this fact about the Lord: He does not change in His *character*, but He will sometimes change His *mind* about what He says He will do. You may need to hear that truth right now. It is a spiritual revelation that *God's character does not change—ever.* However, He has been known to change His mind according to His unwavering mercy.

Mercy is one of God's most outstanding characteristics, and, like Moses's prayers, our prayers should appeal to His character. The Lord is faithful, merciful, loving, compassionate, holy, and just. As Moses did, we can intercede to change God's mind about executing judgment upon the people of the earth. This key principle is revealed throughout the Bible, and I share it throughout the pages of this book. A persistent revival intercessor can help to prepare the way for breakthrough and harvest!

A CRISIS OF UNBELIEF

Let's look at a similar example of Moses's intercession with God from the book of Numbers. The background of this passage is the Israelites' unbelief when the spies were sent to survey the land of Canaan, which God has promised to give them. Ten of the twelve spies brought back a bad report, while Caleb and Joshua brought back a good report. (See Numbers 13:25–33.) The people chose to accept the bad report, grumbling and complaining even to the point of saying, *"Let's appoint a leader and return to Egypt!"* (Numbers 14:4). When Joshua and Caleb tried to reason with them, the people wanted to stone them! (See verses 6–10.) Here is what happened next:

> And the LORD said to Moses, *"How long will this people be disrespectful to Me? And how long will they not believe in Me, despite all the signs that I have performed in their midst? I will strike them with plague and dispossess them, and I will make you into a nation greater and mightier than they."* But Moses said to the LORD, *"Then the Egyptians will hear of it, for by Your strength You brought this people up from their midst, and they will tell it to the inhabitants of this land. They have heard that You, LORD, are in the midst of this people, because You, LORD, are seen eye to eye, while Your cloud stands over them; and You go before them in a pillar of cloud by day, and in a pillar*

of fire by night. Now if You put this people to death all at once, then the nations who have heard of Your fame will say, 'Since the LORD could not bring this people into the land which He promised them by oath, He slaughtered them in the wilderness.'" (Numbers 14:11–16)

God must have really liked Moses because, in a sense, He kept bartering with Moses, wanting to start the nation all over through him. What was happening in this passage? I wonder if God was testing Moses with pride. This seems to be a multilayered incident; if we really take the time to evaluate it, we can see that there were a lot of issues going on in this interaction between God and Moses. If it was a test of pride, then Moses passed it because he continued to choose to intercede on behalf of the Israelites rather than take God's offer to create a new nation from him.

APPEALING TO GOD'S NAME

Once again, Moses pleaded a holy argument before God, saying that the Lord's fame would spread and His great name would be vindicated if He would stay with His people and go before them rather than destroy them.

So now, please, let the power of the Lord be great, just as You have declared, saying, "The LORD is slow to anger and abundant in mercy, forgiving wrongdoing and violation of His Law; but He will by no means leave the guilty unpunished, inflicting the punishment of the fathers on the children to the third and the fourth generations." Please forgive the guilt of this people in accordance with the greatness of Your mercy, just as You also have forgiven this people, from Egypt even until now. (Numbers 14:17–19)

APPEALING TO GOD'S CHARACTER

Moses also cried out for God's power to be revealed. He reminded the Lord that His character does not change—that He is *"slow to anger."* That character trait is also cited in the New Testament as one that we believers should adhere to: *"You know this, my beloved brothers and sisters. Now everyone must be quick to hear, slow to speak, and slow to anger"* (James 1:19). Finally, Moses stood in the gap and confessed the sin of the Israelites as his own: *"Please forgive the guilt of this people in accordance with the greatness of Your mercy"* (Numbers 14:19). Moses is an Old Testament prototype of a New Testament revival intercessor.

> So the LORD said, "I have forgiven them **in accordance with your word**; however, as I live, all the earth will be filled with the glory of the LORD." (Numbers 14:20–21)

Numbers 14:20 is the verse from which I derived the title of this chapter, "When God Listens to the Voice of Man." This Scripture is pivotal for understanding our role in intercession. The Lord answered Moses's plea by saying, *"I have forgiven them in accordance with your word."* Whose word? The word, the prayer, of Moses—the revival intercessor!

I want you to know that we can pray with the same kind of authority—and perhaps even greater authority. We live under the new covenant and the authority that Jesus gave His disciples. (See Matthew 28:17–19.) As an ambassador-intercessor, you can learn to stand in the gap for your family and for your city; you can learn to stand in the gap for your nation in times of chaos and confusion. As you do, the Lord will say to you, as He said to Moses, "I have forgiven them according to your word."

God heard Moses's intercessory plea, and He listened to the voice of a man. In response, pardon was granted instead of judgment meted out.

I get very excited when I think of the mercy and love of God the Father. The fact that the Lord hears us and will change the course of history because of our revival prayers is so profound and seems so crazily extravagant to me that, well, no wonder I'm losing my hair!

After God said He would pardon the people, He released a powerful revelation: *"However, as I live, all the earth will be filled with the glory of the LORD"* (Numbers 14:21). I think this is one of the most significant prophetic declarations in the entire Bible. When one man, Moses, stood in the gap for a breakthrough on behalf of others, and God granted them forgiveness according to Moses's word—when God listened to the voice of a man—God not only gave a pardon, but He also promised to fill the world with His glory!

This means that when God responds to our plea, He does not just hit the delete button to remove the judgment. He also causes a breakthrough by promising that a glory awakening will come upon the earth. The Lord pours forth His heart when He declares, *"All the earth will be filled with the glory of the* LORD.*"* Dear friend, the glory awakening is surely coming because God has prophetically promised it. This prophetic promise was released after a man presented his case before God. May it be so again, and may it be so today with us, in Jesus's name!

SEVEN STEPS TO GOD'S GLORY

As we consider God's promise to fill the earth with His glory, I want to share a pattern I identified in Numbers 14, which I call "Steps to His Glory." I see it as a systematic, seven-point pattern of process and progress. Imagine that we are taking the steps of a stairway or climbing up a ladder rung by rung, moving forward and upward to God's glory.

1. A crisis occurs involving the people's relationship with God. (See Numbers 14:11–12.)

2. We remind God of His covenantal nature. (See Numbers 14:13–17.)

3. We receive and express a divine revelation of His mercy. (See Numbers 14:18.)

4. We impart a desperate cry for forgiveness from this revelation of the divine mercy. (See Numbers 14:19.)

5. God responds to our cry for mercy because *"mercy triumphs over judgment"* (James 2:13). The Lord says that the guilty party is pardoned *"in accordance with your word"* (Numbers 14:20).

6. God releases a prophetic declaration of His glory. (See Numbers 14:21.)

7. The call and the requirements for revival intercession are released and confirmed. The call is for us to enter into the fullness of God's kingdom, following the Lord wholeheartedly and bringing with us a great harvest of souls for God's glory. (See Numbers 14:24.)

When I teach this pattern to people in person, whether at a church or at another venue, as I reveal the process, I physically walk up steps. After moving onto the seventh step, I take one more step up and call everybody forward to participate in a corporate new beginning, rededicating our lives to serving the Lord and being His intercessors on behalf of others. You see, seven is the number of completion, and eight is the number of a new beginning!

WHAT IS OUR RESPONSE?

The consecutive steps we have just reviewed are revealed as parts of the process in which God's glory is released. We must ask ourselves, are these principles true for us today as well? And, if so, what response is needed on our part for the same results to come to pass in our generation, causing God to turn His head earthward?

As I have pondered these principles, I have realized that the Lord responded to Moses's pleas by going from one extreme of judgment to the other extreme of pardon, while also declaring a profound prophetic destiny involving the entire earth. What moved the heart of God in this pendulum swing?

Remember that in Numbers 14:19, Moses made his appeal for pardon not on the basis of the people's merit but on the basis of God's great mercy. Moses had a revelation that *the Father's heart was one of mercy*. Revival breakthrough comes when we realize that *we can never earn mercy, but God freely offers His mercy to us*. Mercy already exists in God's heart, and He is looking for a people who will come in alignment with the higher law of the nature of His heart.

Moses also saw that God's mercy was *continual*. This is a huge truth. It's easy to believe that God's mercy is occasional, but do you really believe that God's mercy is constant, not given merely intermittently? Let's look again at Numbers 14:19: "*You have also forgiven this people, from Egypt even until now.*"

HOW DOES BREAKTHROUGH COME?

What will it take to change the mind (not the character) of God in this generation to avert judgment for its rebellion and sin? To change the mind of God, we must *change our own character and mindset to align with His*. In this regard, let us review two vital Scriptures:

Jesus Christ is the same yesterday and today, and forever.

(Hebrews 13:8)

We must realize, in a fundamental way, that God's nature is always the same and that Jesus is an exact representation of the Father. Thus, what moved God's heart yesterday will move God's heart again today.

For judgment will be merciless to one who has shown no mercy; mercy triumphs over judgment. (James 2:13)

If you want mercy, you must give mercy. There is always a higher spiritual dimension in which to walk. Look up into the Father's heart. Deep in the center of His bosom is the heart of mercy, and mercy always triumphs over judgment. Therefore, align yourself with the nature of God's heart, and you will *receive* the nature of God's heart; align yourself with a cry for God's mercy to be poured out on others.

Yes, even today, God wants to bend His heart and His ear earthward and release His mercy. Perhaps He's waiting for you. When He hears His heart beating in an earthen vessel or within a remnant in the body of Christ, we will see the same results once again. The Father will listen to the voice of people whose pleas echo what is in agreement with His heart. Therefore, let mercy triumph over judgment again, again, and again. Let the cry for mercy arise!

Psalm 107:28 says, "*Then they cried out to the LORD in their trouble, and He brought them out of their distresses.*" The nations of the world are in a time of great distress, but our God is the same yesterday, today, and forever. I believe that this temporary darkness is but the great backdrop that will allow His light to shine and rulers to come into the brightness of its shining. (See Isaiah 60:1–3.)

SEVEN STEPS TO BECOMING AN EFFECTIVE INTERCESSOR

Now that we have identified the primary characteristics of revival intercessors and seen examples of the types of prayers they offer to God, let's look at how you can become an effective intercessor who is preparing for revival breakthrough that will impact your world for God's glory!

1. Passionately pursue God Himself through prayer, often with fasting. Walk out a total, heartfelt commitment to the Lord Jesus Christ, His church, and His purposes. (A thorough teaching on fasting is coming up in part 2 of this book.)

2. Carry a heart full of compassion and love for His people and for His plans to be fulfilled in your generation.

3. Regularly take time for worship and praise, and schedule periods of solitude in order to hear God's voice.

4. Actively read and meditate on the Bible, asking God to enable you to experience everything in His Word that declares your inheritance in Christ Jesus.

5. Read inspiring autobiographies and biographies of dedicated believers, including books that recount missionary journeys.

   For example, I recommend *A Diary of Signs and Wonders* by Maria Woodworth-Etter; *Rees Howells: Intercessor* by Norman Grubb; *The Light and the Glory* by Peter Marshall and David Manuel; and *No Easy Road* by Dick Eastman, which I have read at least ten times. Each time I have read *No Easy Road*, I have found another nugget that has touched my praying heart, such as how Father Daniel Nash gave himself totally to being Charles Finney's personal intercessor during the Second Great Awakening.

6. Develop tools to help others cultivate a lifestyle of prayer and intercession.

   I once met an older gentleman who was part of Martha Wing Robinson's healing revival move of the Spirit in Zion, Illinois, at the same time as John Alexander Dowie's ministry in the early twentieth century. This healing revival was known for the manifest presence of God. I visited Zion and studied about Robinson's life. When this older gentleman moved to Kansas City, I used to sit with him and ask him questions because he had also attended meetings led by A. A. Allen, Jack Coe, and other revivalists. When I would start to ask questions that were too specific, he would not answer. Rather, tears would come to his eyes, and he would always veer the conversation back to saying, "Oh, that Man, Christ Jesus." That is a revivalist—one who deeply loves Jesus. From my various revival studies, the time I spent learning from this gentleman, and my own experiences, I have developed tools for intercession that I am now able to share with you.

7. Love doing it! Revival intercessors are not just hearers of the Word of God; they are also doers of the Word. (See James 1:22–25.)

Jason Ford, the director of our GEM Prayer Shield ministry, and his assistant, Susan Carter, love our invitation-only prayer calls even more than I do. They kick into gear on every prayer call, every time! Bob Perry, who, along with Peggy Adams, heads up Market Place Prayer in Nashville, and many others, are also on fire. And there are passionate intercessors like these in every major city! Each of these individuals is committed to doing what they are commissioned to do as a revival intercessor. They love praying and calling forth breakthrough for people, places, and situations.

YEARNING FOR GOD'S PRESENCE

Let's conclude this chapter by looking at one other intercessory prayer of Moses:

*Then Moses said to the LORD, "See, You say to me, 'Bring up this people!' But You Yourself have not let me know whom You will send with me. Moreover, You have said, 'I have known you by name, and you have also found favor in My sight.' Now then, if I have found favor in Your sight in any way, please let me know Your ways so that I may know You, in order that I may find favor in Your sight. Consider too, that this nation is Your people." And He said, "My presence shall go with you, and I will give you rest." Then he said to Him, "**If Your presence does not go with us, do not lead us up from here.** For how then can it be known that I have found favor in Your sight, I and Your people? Is it not by Your going with us, so that we, I and Your people, may be distinguished from all the other people who are on the face of the earth?"* (Exodus 33:12–16)

This is a great prayer about the presence of God. Moses contends for the Lord's attendance among His people. In current-day vernacular, he is saying, "Hey, listen, God. If You're going to send me, then You need to go along with us because, without You, we have no outstanding or distinguishing characteristics as the people of God. It is only Your presence that makes us known as Your children."

Likewise, for Christians today, it's not necessarily going to be our vocabulary, our dress, or even our customs and traditions that distinguish us as God's people. What identifies us as children of God the Father is *His abiding presence!*

That, my fellow believer, is what revival breakthrough is all about: experiencing the manifestation of God's presence—both among us and within us—and living in its ongoing reality. Are you a carrier of His presence? That is what Moses was contending for: *"If Your presence does not go with us, do not lead us up from here."*

Theologian and preacher A. W. Tozer (1897–1963) stated, "If the Holy Spirit was withdrawn from the church today, 95 percent of what we do would go on and no one would know the difference. If the Holy Spirit had been withdrawn from the New Testament church, 95 percent of what they did would stop, and everybody would know the difference."[13] That was a pretty sad commentary from Tozer regarding the church in his day.

Today, let us be a church that welcomes the Holy Spirit into our hearts and our everyday lives. Let us be like Moses and cry out for God's presence to be released and to go before us. May the "forerunner spirit" be poured out upon us again as revival intercessors, and may the church be filled with, led by, and captured by the loveliness of the Lord's great presence.

LET'S PRAY TOGETHER

Heavenly Father, as we continue our journey toward revival breakthrough, we commit ourselves to You once again. Here we are; we are Yours. We have been bought by the price of the blood of the Lamb of God on the cross of Calvary. We desire to learn from

---

13. https://www.goodreads.com/quotes/964813-if-the-holy-spirit-was-withdrawn-from-the-church-today.

those who have blazed the trail before us. We want to discover the path that leads to a greater manifestation of God's glory on earth. We desire to offer prayers that are in alignment with Your very heart. We want to be voices that matter and that can be heard in the courts of heaven. Teach us and lead us so that true, lasting revival will come into our lives, our families, our cities, and our nations. In Jesus's great name, Amen and Amen!

3

IDENTIFICATIONAL REPENTANCE: FATHER, FORGIVE US!

"I prayed to the LORD my God and confessed, and said, 'Oh, Lord, the great and awesome God, who keeps His covenant and faithfulness for those who love Him and keep His commandments, we have sinned, we have done wrong, and acted wickedly and rebelled, even turning aside from Your commandments and ordinances.'"
—Daniel 9:4–5

One September morning in 1991, while my wife, Michal Ann, and I were ministering in the Big Apple, specifically in Queens, I heard from the Lord. As was the custom in my relationship with the Holy Spirit during that period of time, as I would rest and linger early in the morning, the voice of the Lord would speak clearly to me. This time, He spoke these words: "I will release new understandings of identification and intercession whereby the legal basis of the rights of the demonic powers of the air to remain will be removed."[14]

I had been reading portions of Scripture in Daniel, Nehemiah, and Ezra, along with the Lord's Prayer. I had also been reading books by

---

14. James W. Goll, *Father, Forgive Us* (Shippensburg, PA: Destiny Image Publishers, 1999), 21.

C. Peter Wagner, Rees Howells, and David Yonggi Cho, as well as Wesley L. Duewel's book *Mighty Prevailing Prayer*. After hearing from the Lord that early morning in September, in one moment, all my research and readings on prayer completely came together. That revelation—"I will release new understandings of *identification* and *intercession* whereby the legal basis of the rights of the demonic powers of the air to remain will be removed"— opened volumes of understanding to me. I pray the same will be true for you.

Perhaps you are well-versed in the spiritual terminology of intercessory prayer. However, if you are not, "identificational repentance," and a related term, "identification intercession," might be new expressions for you. Because revelation is progressive, as we grow in our faith and as we grow in any area of life in doctrine and in teaching, we grow in our vocabulary as well. In this chapter, you will learn the meaning of these terms and discover how they apply to your prayer life.

Our Scripture theme comes from Daniel's prayer in which he asked God to forgive His people in exile. Daniel wrote that he *"prayed to the LORD [his] God and confessed, and said, 'Oh, Lord, the great and awesome God, who keeps His covenant and faithfulness for those who love Him and keep His commandments, we have sinned, we have done wrong, and acted wickedly and rebelled, even turning aside from Your commandments and ordinances'"* (Daniel 9:4–5).

Daniel didn't pray, "*I* sinned," and he didn't say, "*They* sinned." Daniel identified with his people, expressing, "*We* have sinned, *we* have done wrong, *we* have acted wickedly and rebelled, *we* have even turned aside from Your commandments and ordinances." As we dig deeper into this teaching on identificational repentance, let us pray together that God would open our hearts to what He wants us to understand about this essential area of prayer.

Lord, in order for revival breakthrough to happen, we need hearts that not only see the need for forgiveness but also fully identify with our families, neighborhoods, and nations. Jesus, Your disciples asked You to instruct them in how to pray. In the model prayer You gave them, You said, "Our Father...forgive us...." As the spotless, sinless Lamb of God, You obviously didn't need forgiveness—yet those were Your words as You included Your disciples in Your prayer. This lesson on effective praying wasn't about You—it was about others. *They* needed forgiveness, and You were showing grace and mercy so Your disciples could learn to do the same for those around them. Father God, I pray that You would do that kind of work in us today, even right now. Holy Spirit, if You would do that, I know that we could take another step toward true revival breakthrough. Amen and Amen.

FATHER, FORGIVE US!

When I pray, I dialogue with my heavenly Father, and, throughout this book, I am taking you along into my conversational prayer journey. When I ask the Lord a question, it usually prompts me to ask other questions that ultimately lead me to His answer.

One such example relates to what we just prayed about in regard to Jesus's model prayer, commonly known as the Lord's Prayer. Jesus said, *"Our Father...forgive us."* Since Jesus was without sin, why did He include that phrase using the word *"our"*? That's what I asked the Lord one day: "Jesus, is there something else behind this particular word usage?" That idea led me to wonder, "Is there something more behind the words that Daniel used in his own prayer? Is there something about the heart that can replace self-righteousness with mercy for other people?" The Lord's answer: yes!

Let's look more closely at what Jesus taught His disciples about prayer and forgiveness:

And when you pray, you shall not be like the hypocrites. For they love to pray standing in the synagogues and on the corners of the streets, that they may be seen by men. Assuredly, I say to you, they have their reward. But you, when you pray, go into your room, and when you have shut your door, pray to your Father who is in the secret place; and your Father who sees in secret will reward you openly. And when you pray, do not use vain repetitions as the heathen do. For they think that they will be heard for their many words. Therefore do not be like them. For your Father knows the things you have need of before you ask Him.

In this manner, therefore, pray: Our Father in heaven, hallowed be Your name. Your kingdom come. Your will be done, on earth as it is in heaven. Give us this day our daily bread. And forgive us our debts, as we forgive our debtors. And do not lead us into temptation, but deliver us from the evil one. For Yours is the kingdom and the power and the glory forever. Amen. For if you forgive men their offenses, your heavenly Father will also forgive you. But if you do not forgive men their offenses, neither will your Father forgive your offenses.

(Matthew 6:5–15)

The disciples were in great need of a revelation about prayer. After observing Jesus's prayer life, they told Jesus that John the Baptist had taught his disciples how to pray, and they would now like Him to teach them. In response, Jesus didn't give them a line-by-line rote way to pray, saying, "Repeat after Me...." Rather, He gave them prayer *themes: "In this manner, therefore, pray...."*

I'm not saying that it's wrong to repeat the words of the Lord's Prayer, but that wasn't Jesus's intention when He taught His disciples how to pray. I believe He was giving them a model with topics they were to use when praying *"in this manner."* In this way, they would absorb the essence and substance of the prayer into their hearts, minds, and spirits.

Again, Jesus's prayer began, *"Our Father...."* Now, that's a revelation! Jesus didn't say, "My Father...." Like Daniel, He was including others in His prayer to God the Father. In the same way, in revival intercession, we stand in the gap for our families, our cities, our nations, and the people of the world.

Our prayer is for God's will to be done on earth as it is in heaven:

May God's will be done in our family, in Nashville, in London, in Hong Kong, in the United States, in Australia, in South Africa, and throughout the planet Earth. Give us today our daily bread in schools, hospitals, skyscrapers, warehouses near and far. Forgive us in our homes and in boardrooms, churches, legislatures, and offices of heads of state. Forgive our debts, Lord, as we forgive our debtors who have been affected by our selfishness. Point out our wrongs to us so we may make amends. Lead us not into temptation when faced with the myriad of sins and fleshly pleasures that are rife in this world. Deliver us—all of us—from the evil one, whose main goal is to prevent revival and to destroy any attempt at breakthrough.

That's devotional praying—that's praying in like manner.

Are you getting the idea? Identificational repentance and identificational intercession are not just terms we say but realities we put into practice. They refer to a process by which we come to truly identify with people and strive to reach them through the compassionate heart of God. There's heart behind our words in such prayers.

Let's build on this greatly needed revelation of identification, realizing that we must clear out the debris and remove obstacles, getting them out of the way so God's people may be free to serve Him and heal the world around them.

In recent days and years, I have tended to use the term "ambassadorial prayer" because it seems to be phrase that is a bit more understandable for most people. But for now, let's continue to investigate what this all means.

THE MEANING OF IDENTIFICATION

The following are significant quotes from biblical scholars who have eloquently defined some of the concepts that are germane to our discussion. Many other people have researched and written on this topic, but the words of these particular teachers have impacted me directly.[15]

Dr. Gary Greig, a former associate professor of Hebrew and Old Testament at Regent University's School of Divinity, has done extensive study in the area of prayer for revival and identificational repentance. Dr. Greig states,

The deepest scheme is the enemy's attempt to keep hidden the defilement of the land through historic sins and the enemy's

---

15. I have compiled many such teachings, as well as my writings on the subject, building on topics that complement each other. For example, in my book Strike the Mark (New Kensington, PA: Whitaker House, 2019), I include a chapter entitled "Confessing Generational Sin," which even more thoroughly examines this practice. I encourage you to visit my website, godencounters.com, if a particular topic in this book piques your interest, as there may be additional, more in-depth books or webinars available for you.

attempt to keep the Church from its priestly role of asking God to forgive these sins and of leading the way and repenting of these sins that have defiled the land, grieved God's heart, and empowered the enemy here."[16]

I simply add a loud and confirming "Amen" to this brilliant theological statement.

Cindy Jacobs, a dear friend and colleague, is an author and the cofounder of Generals of Intercession, now called Generals International. She brings us additional understanding of this formerly neglected area of teaching, stating, "Remitting of sins is not something that has been widely taught or understood in the past, but which we are now coming to understand as a vital part of our spiritual warfare. Jesus modeled this principle on the cross when He said, 'Father forgive them, for they do not know what they do' (Luke 23:34)."[17]

As I pursued this concept of corporately identifying with a need and then further identifying with a proper response—moving from "me" to "us" in identificational repentance—I discovered that it was John Dawson, a wordsmith of years ago, who may have first brought that terminology to us. There were many others, but I thank the Lord for John as a forerunner in this vein of thought. In his powerful book *Healing America's Wounds*, John explains with detailed examples, possibly more than anyone else, the importance of identificational confession and intercession:

> If we have broken our covenants with God and violated our relationships with one another, the path to reconciliation must begin with the act of confession. The greatest wounds in human history, the greatest injustices, have not happened through the acts of some individual perpetrator, rather through the institutions, systems, philosophies, cultures, religions and governments of mankind. Because of this, we, as individuals, are tempted to absolve ourselves of all individual responsibility.

16. Dr. Gary Greig, "Praying for Revival: Focusing Our Intercession, Spiritual Warfare and Protecting Ourselves in the Battle," teaching outline (Virginia Beach, VA: Regent University, 1996).
17. Cindy Jacobs, "Identificational Repentance Through Biblical Remitting of Sins," in *Releasing Destiny* by Stephen Mansfield (Nashville TN: Daniel 1 School of Leadership, n.d.).

Unless somebody identifies themselves with corporate entities, such as the nation of our citizenship, or the subculture of our ancestors, the act of honest confession will never take place. This leaves us in a world of injury and offense in which no corporate sin is ever acknowledged, reconciliation never begins and old hatreds deepen.

The followers of Jesus are to step into this impasse as agents of healing. Within our ranks are representatives of every category of humanity. Trembling in our heavenly Father's presence, we see clearly the sins of humankind and have no inclination to cover them up. Thus, we are called to live out the biblical practice of identificational repentance, a neglected truth that opens the floodgates of revival and brings healing to the nations.[18]

THE PROCESS OF IDENTIFICATION IN INTERCESSION

Now that we know what identificational repentance is, let us narrow the topic a little to focus more on "identification in intercession." This is the wedding, or convergence, of the spirit of revelation and the spirit of conviction,[19] as we see in these two Scripture passages:

*That the God of our Lord Jesus Christ, the Father of glory, may give you a **spirit of wisdom and of revelation** in the knowledge of Him. I pray that the eyes of your heart may be enlightened, so that you will know what is the hope of His calling, what are the riches of the glory of His inheritance in the saints.* (Ephesians 1:17–18)

*But I tell you the truth: it is to your advantage that I am leaving; for if I do not leave, the Helper will not come to you; but if I go, I will send Him to you. And He, **when He comes, will convict** the world regarding sin, and righteousness, and judgment.* (John 16:7–8)

The spirit of revelation imparts wisdom and insight regarding the nature, the degree, and the depth of national and even generational sin.

18. John Dawson, *Healing America's Wounds* (Ventura, CA: Regal Books, 1994), 30.
19. In an upcoming chapter, we will look at the five classic characteristics of revival, one being the experiential conviction of sin.

Then the spirit of conviction awakens us with a deep identificational burden for our sins before God, provoking a desperate desire for confession, repentance, and forgiveness.

The revelation and convergence give birth to a heart cry for the removal of the hindrances—a removal of the obstacles of sin that block the fullness of spiritual awakening. That's what the corporeity, or identifying, is about with regard to confessing generational sins.

> And it will be said: "Build up, build up, prepare the road! **Remove the obstacles** out of the way of **my people**." (Isaiah 57:14 NIV)

> The voice of one calling out, "**Clear the way for the LORD** in the wilderness; make straight in the desert a highway for our God." (Isaiah 40:3)

> As it is written in the book of the words of Isaiah the prophet: "A voice of one calling in the wilderness, '**Prepare the way for the Lord**, make straight paths for him.'" (Luke 3:4–5 NIV)

I love the fact that these principles are introduced in the Old Testament and that Jesus brings them forward into the New Testament as the One who comes to us along straight paths in the name of the Lord.

Isaiah 57:14 says, "*Remove the obstacles out of the way of my people*" (NIV). Isaiah 40:3 and Luke 3:4 say it another way: "*Clear the way for the LORD*" and "*Prepare the way for the Lord*." The two intents are similar but are actually pointing out and removing the hindrances, or obstacles, for two different parties—God's people and the Lord. Both actions are needed for effective intercession.

The wedding of the spirit of revelation and the spirit of conviction allows us to identify with the needs of other people to such an extent that we understand their heart, and we become one in heart with them. We don't talk *at* someone, we talk *with* someone.

In identifying with the present-day sinful condition of our generation, we are following the model of our Lord Jesus Christ. Jesus took the sin of all humankind upon the cross of Calvary. By the spirit of revelation and conviction, the burden of the Lord can come upon us as believers. Then we pick it up and carry it away in prayer to God's throne on behalf of others.

By choosing to lay aside our own position and identify with others, our hearts are burdened by the Spirit of God. Such prayer has gone well past merely changing our terminology from "I" to "we." Rather, their burdens, their hearts, their desires, and their needs become ours. When this happens, it is one of the earmarks of the beginning of widespread revival!

FIVE ESSENTIALS FOR IDENTIFICATION AND INTERCESSION

I have found that five essentials are needed for us to be able to walk in identification and intercession. We need to be a people who…

1. are willing to look at others with wide-open eyes.

2. are willing to give up our own lives for the sake of God's will.

3. have broken hearts for others.

4. have grace to carry the burdens of others.

5. are desperate and willing to be the answer to our own prayers.

For a long time, I've been pondering a new term: *ambassadorial intercession*. In chapter two, I said that you can learn to be an ambassador-intercessor. We are, in fact, ambassadors for Christ with a mission to touch people's lives with His message. We are missionaries, sent out to other peoples to shine God's light in their lives. If you're a successful ambassador, your heart sees the hearts of others, and you can identify with their role in God's plan. As an ambassador of intercession, you're sent to a people group, to a cause, and you absorb this group or cause into your life, for Jesus's sake.

THREE ASPECTS OF AMBASSADORIAL INTERCESSION

As we learn to identify with others and their needs, we need to carefully consider three important aspects of ambassadorial intercession: (1) *the act of confessing,* (2) *the state of being convicted,* and (3) *the condition of being convinced,* which closely follows conviction. Let's look at these areas more closely.

THE ACT OF CONFESSING

What does it mean to confess? There are two different Greek words that are translated "to confess" in the New Testament:

1. *Homologeó*. Among the meanings of this word are "to speak the same," "to agree," "to profess (confess)," "to declare," and "to admit."[20] This word is used, for example, in 1 John 1:9: *"If we confess [homologeó] our sins, He is faithful and righteous, so that He will forgive us our sins and cleanse us from all unrighteousness."* The Scriptures say that if we confess, if we profess, if we declare, if we admit our sins, God will forgive us for those sins.

2. *Exomologeó*. This word variously means "to agree," "to confess," "to consent fully," "to agree out and out," "to confess," "to admit," and "to acknowledge."[21] James 5:16 tells us, *"Therefore, confess [exomologeó] your sins to one another, and pray for one another so that you may be healed."* Thus, there can be private confession, but there can also be public or corporate confession.

Both of these words carry a sense of agreement. To confess our sins means to agree with God regarding sin—our own sin as well as other people's sin. We agree that we have done wrong, that our thoughts, words, and actions have not reflected God's holy and loving character.

BEING CONVICTED AND CONVINCED

Next, what does it mean to be convicted so that we are convinced? Let's look at the following Greek word for "convict":

Elegchó. Among the meanings of this word are "to expose," "to convict," "to reprove," "to rebuke," "to discipline," and "to show to be guilty."[22]

---

20. *Strong's Exhaustive Concordance of the Bible*, #3670, https://www.biblehub.com/greek/3670.htm.
21. *Strong's*, #1843, https://biblehub.com/greek/1843.htm.
22. *Strong's*, #1651, https://biblehub.com/greek/1651.htm.

We find this term in John 16:8, which we looked at earlier in this chapter. Jesus declared, *"And He* [the Holy Spirit], *when He comes, will convict the world regarding sin, and righteousness, and judgment."* It is the role of the Holy Spirit to convict us of God's truth.

The dictionary also gives some excellent definitions of *conviction* in the sense we are discussing: "a strong persuasion or belief"; "the state of being convinced"; "the act of convincing a person of error or of compelling the admission of a truth"; "the state of being convinced of error or compelled to admit the truth."[23]

Being convicted regarding God's Word and ways is the opposite of being wishy-washy about one's beliefs and about wrongdoing. In the broad context of our study, we can say that "conviction" is a values-based principle and motivation to stand strong for your beliefs. You know who you are and what you believe—you hold the conviction that God is the Ruler of your life and also of the whole world.

To be convicted is be both *convinced* and *compelled.* Again, the verb "to convict" means to find or prove to be guilty, to convince of error or sinfulness. When we are convicted about a sin, we don't merely verbalize or admit the wrong. Instead, we deeply acknowledge our guilt and make a profession of responsibility regarding it because our heart is absolutely convinced of the reality or the horror of that sin, whether it be personal or corporate.

In one biblical example, Daniel laments all the sins he and his people have committed. He has been convicted of them and confesses them in verse after verse in the ninth chapter of Daniel, part of which I shared earlier. He details sins and rightfully admits to the Lord how "we" have done wrong, identifying with Israel and accepting their sins as his:

> I prayed to the LORD my God and confessed, and said, "Oh, Lord, the great and awesome God, who keeps His covenant and faithfulness for those who love Him and keep His commandments, **we have sinned, we have done wrong**, and acted wickedly and rebelled, even turning aside from Your commandments and ordinances. Moreover, we have not listened to Your servants the prophets, who spoke in Your name to our

---

23. *Merriam-Webster.com Dictionary*, s.v. "conviction," https://www.merriam-webster.com/dictionary/conviction.

kings, our leaders, our fathers, and all the people of the land…. Open shame belongs to us, LORD, to our kings, our leaders, and our fathers, because we have sinned against You. To the Lord our God belong compassion and forgiveness, because we have rebelled against Him; and we have not obeyed the voice of the LORD our God, to walk in His teachings which He set before us through His servants the prophets. Indeed, all Israel has violated Your Law and turned aside, not obeying Your voice; so the curse has gushed forth on us, along with the oath which is written in the Law of Moses the servant of God, because we have sinned against Him…. So now, our God, listen to the prayer of Your servant and to his pleas, and for Your sake, Lord, let Your face shine on Your desolate sanctuary. My God, incline Your ear and hear! Open Your eyes and see our desolations and the city which is called by Your name; for we are not presenting our pleas before You based on any merits of our own, but based on Your great compassion. Lord, hear! Lord, forgive! Lord, listen and take action! For Your own sake, my God, do not delay, because Your city and Your people are called by Your name." (Daniel 9:4–6, 8–11, 17–19)

And consider how Nehemiah took it upon himself to acknowledge his conviction and thereby confess his and his family's sins, along with the sins of the people, praying:

Please, LORD God of heaven, the great and awesome God, who keeps the covenant and faithfulness for those who love Him and keep His commandments: let Your ear now be attentive and Your eyes open, to hear the prayer of Your servant which I am praying before You now, day and night, on behalf of the sons of Israel Your servants, confessing the sins of the sons of Israel which we have committed against You; **I and my father's house** *have sinned. We have acted very corruptly against You and have not kept the commandments, nor the statutes, nor the ordinances which You commanded Your servant Moses…. They are Your servants and Your people whom You redeemed by Your great power and by Your strong hand. Please, Lord, may Your ear be attentive to the prayer of Your servant and the prayer of Your servants who delight to revere Your name, and please make Your* *servant successful today and grant him mercy before this man.*

(Nehemiah 1:5–7, 10–11)

In a third example, notice the corporate nature of Ezra's prayer—and the corporate response:

*I said, "My God, I am ashamed and humiliated to lift up my face to You, my God, for **our wrongful deeds** have risen above our heads, and **our guilt** has grown even to the heavens. **Since the days of our fathers** to this day we have been in great guilt, and because of our wrongful deeds we, our kings, and our priests have been handed over to the kings of the lands…." Now while Ezra was praying and making confession, weeping and prostrating himself before the house of God, **a very large assembly, men, women, and children, gathered** to him from Israel; for the people wept greatly.*   (Ezra 9:6–7; 10:1)

Specific issues are mentioned in the Bible regarding generational sins that must be addressed:

+ Idolatry

+ Temples to pagan religions

+ Murder and the shedding of innocent blood

+ Witchcraft

+ Adultery

+ Sodomy

+ Sexual perversion

I have studied the subject of identificational repentance for years and have been blessed to take its message around the world. I've written about it too in a forerunner book that was originally published as *Father, Forgive Us* and that later became an expanded edition entitled *Intercession: The Power and the Passion to Shape History*. In that book, I identify five major historic wrongs in the history of the United States:

+ The enslavement of multitudes of Blacks

+ The displacement and genocide of the First Nations (indigenous, tribal groups)

- The persecution and genocide of the Jewish people (including denying refuge to European Jews attempting to escape the Nazi threat)

- The denial of suffrage to Blacks and women

- Abortion, by wedding the god of mammon and Molech

To the above lists of intercessory needs, I would add some of today's maladies, which have adversely affected multiple generations, such as the removal of the Ten Commandments, prayer, and Bible reading from our public schools; substance abuse (alcohol, illegal drugs, and so forth); rioting; anger and rage; hatred; cursing; and unforgiveness.

Another issue that should be addressed and confessed is the prevalence of pornography, which may be routinely seen on television, on movie screens, and on magazine covers—even those that can be seen while standing in line at the grocery-store checkout. And, by the way, there are no "50 shades of gray"—there is only black-and-white. We have become numb to pornography because it is so commonly displayed in our society. Pastors today should be crying out to God on behalf of our nations, as did Daniel, Nehemiah, and Ezra.

All of these wrongs, and more, have been topics of my research for many years—and all relate to this chapter's theme. Other wrongs may come to your mind as you continue to read. Let's continue to look with fresh eyes at the need for identificational repentance. *Father, forgive us.*

ARISE TO THE CHALLENGE

C. Peter Wagner, a dear brother who is now with the Lord, was one of this past generation's generals in God's army. He had great expertise in biblical research and spiritual terminology, and he was a pioneer in spiritual warfare and missiology—defined as personal and spiritual growth combined with missions, discipleship, and evangelism. We find the following helpful insights in his book *Warfare Prayer*:

> Suppose demonic strongholds actually exist in a nation or a city, affecting society in general and resistance to the gospel in particular. What can be done about it? Just as in the case of demonized individuals, if sin is present, repentance is called for. If curses are

in effect, they need to be broken, and if emotional scars are causing pain, inner healing is needed.

We know from the Old Testament that nations can be guilty of corporate sins. This was not only true of Gentile nations but of Israel as well. Both Nehemiah and Daniel give us examples of godly persons who felt the burden for the sins of their nations.... It is important to note that both Nehemiah and Daniel, while they were standing before God on behalf of their entire nation, confessed not only the corporate sins of their people, but also their individual sins. Those who remit the sins of nations must not fail to identify personally with the sins that were or are being committed, even though they might not personally be as guilty of them as some other sins.[24]

Again, identificational repentance and confession do not only involve a change in terminology. Neither do they mean just reading history books about repentance and revivals in the lives of past believers. They require receiving a deep revelation of identification, accompanied by developing a heart connection with the people involved and their needs. It's a convergence of the spirit of revelation and the spirit of conviction. As C. Peter Wagner wrote, "Those who remit the sins of nations must not fail to identify personally with the sins that were or are being committed."

Even though we might not personally be as guilty as others regarding particular sins, we still have to take the log out of our own eye before we can take the speck out of someone else's eye. (See, for example, Matthew 7:1–5.) In many churches, at times, there are big logs of self-righteousness and intolerance. Oh, Lord, forgive us. We need revival!

THE POWER OF THE BLOOD FOR REVIVAL

Ultimately, revival comes upon an individual or a people through the blood of Jesus, which was shed on the cross for every human being. We must acknowledge our utter dependence on Jesus to initiate and complete the work of identificational repentance and intercession within us. A few confirming Scriptures from God's Word reveal these truths:

24. C. Peter Wagner, *Warfare Prayer* (Ventura, CA, Regal Books, 1992), 130–131.

But now in Christ Jesus you who previously were far away have been brought near by the blood of Christ. (Ephesians 2:13)

Therefore, brothers and sisters, since we have confidence to enter the holy place by the blood of Jesus.... (Hebrews 10:19)

Therefore Jesus also suffered outside the gate, that He might sanctify the people through His own blood.... Now may the God of peace, who brought up from the dead the great Shepherd of the sheep through the blood of the eternal covenant, that is, Jesus our Lord.... (Hebrews 13:12, 20)

If we walk in the Light as He Himself is in the Light, we have fellowship with one another, and the blood of Jesus His Son cleanses us from all sin. (1 John 1:7)

And from Jesus Christ, the faithful witness, the firstborn of the dead, and the ruler of the kings of the earth. To Him who loves us and released us from our sins by His blood.... (Revelation 1:5)

Although the following hymn was written in the 1800s, it is still sung today throughout the world because of the eternal truth about Jesus's blood contained in its lyrics. Feel free to sing or hum along while you read the words:

Would you be free from your burden of sin?
There's power in the blood, power in the blood
Would you o'er evil the victory win?
There's wonderful power in the blood

Would you be whiter, much whiter than snow?
There's power in the blood, power in the blood
Sin stains are lost in its life-giving flow
There's wonderful power in the blood

Would you do service for Jesus your King?
There's power in the blood, power in the blood
Would you live daily His praises to sing?
There's wonderful power in the blood

Lord, how we need Your power
Every day and every hour
Lord, how we need Your power
Every day and every hour

Lord how we need Your
Power, power, wonder-working power
In the blood of the Lamb
Power, power, wonder-working power
In the precious blood of the Lamb.[25]

Let us receive the power of Jesus's blood in our lives as we pray the following prayer:

Father, we cleanse our hands with the blood of Jesus. We apply the blood of Jesus to our eyes, Lord, so that we might see into the spiritual realm...with clarity. We apply the blood of Jesus to our ears to cleanse our ears of any defilement, wickedness, garbage, gossip, or slander that has been poured into our ears so that we might hear clearly what You are speaking to us. We apply the blood of Jesus to our lips and to our tongues so that You would be able to cleanse us of all those things we have spoken that really haven't been of You at all. Father, we apply the blood of Jesus to our heart and our minds. So, Father, we ask You to put the blood of Jesus on our hearts, our thoughts, and our emotions, and to cleanse our minds from dead works so that we might serve the living God.

Father, we apply the blood of Jesus to our feet. Cleanse us from the corruption in the world and from the dust of the world. Father, cleanse us of those places that we've walked in that really haven't been ordered of You. Lord, we receive the words of the Bible where, in Psalm 37:23 [New Living Translation], it says, "*The LORD directs the steps of the godly. He delights in every detail of their lives.*" We will

---

25. Lewis Edgar Jones, "There Is Power in the Blood," 1899.

have holy steps, walking on that highway of holiness. Praise You, Lord! And we ask that You would cleanse us from the top of our heads to the soles of our feet. Thank You, Lord![26]

IF WE WILL, HE WILL

We—God's children, His people—have a responsibility to prompt or provoke revival breakthrough through our prayers. Biblical examples of this principle include the following Scriptures, one of which we have already reviewed in this chapter:

> **If My people** who are called by My name will humble themselves, and pray and seek My face, and turn from their wicked ways, **then I will** hear from heaven, and will forgive their sin and heal their land.
>
> (2 Chronicles 7:14 NKJV)

Our greatest opportunity is that *if we will* humble ourselves and pray, *then God will* hear, forgive, and heal. He is able, and He is more than willing, to do so.

> And lead us not into temptation, but deliver us from evil.
>
> (Matthew 6:13 KJV)

The Lord is our Deliverer. Let us call upon Him for our every need.

> Now, our God, listen to the prayer of Your servant and to his pleas, and for Your sake, Lord, let Your face shine on Your desolate sanctuary. My God, incline Your ear and hear! Open Your eyes and see our desolations and the city which is called by Your name.
>
> (Daniel 9:17–18)

We need God's face to shine upon our desolate land. The greatest destiny of the church and of every nation—our nation—could be right in front of our eyes. For when we cry, "Father, forgive us," He comes running to our aid. So, don't be dismayed by the state of your life, your country, or the world. Instead, cry out to your heavenly Father, "Forgive Your people and their land!"

---

26. Goll, *Father, Forgive Us*, 232–33.

PRAYER PRECEDES REVIVAL

Prayer precedes the outpouring of the Spirit, and I believe that, in part 1 of this book, we have covered a lot of important territory regarding this aspect of *Revival Breakthrough*. The following are several Scripture passages that confirm God's listening ear and compassionate heart toward us—how He responds to the prayers and cries of His children. As we move on to part 2, I encourage you to read and reflect on these Scriptures:

> **God heard their groaning and he remembered** *his covenant with Abraham, with Isaac and with Jacob. So God looked on the Israelites and was concerned about them.* (Exodus 2:24–25 NIV)

> *In you our ancestors put their trust; they trusted and you delivered them. To you* **they cried out and were saved;** *in you they trusted and were not put to shame.* (Psalm 22:4–5 NIV)

> *Midian so impoverished the Israelites that they* **cried out to the LORD** *for help. When the Israelites* **cried out to the LORD** *because of Midian,* **he sent them a prophet....** (Judges 6:6–8 NIV)

> *Then Samuel took a suckling lamb and sacrificed it as a whole burnt offering to the LORD. He* **cried out to the LORD** *on Israel's behalf, and* **the LORD answered him.** (1 Samuel 7:9 NIV)

> *Put on sackcloth, you priests, and mourn; wail, you who minister before the altar. Come, spend the night in sackcloth, you who minister before my God; for the grain offerings and drink offerings are withheld from the house of your God. Declare a holy fast; call a sacred assembly. Summon the elders and all who live in the land to the house of the LORD your God, and* **cry out to the LORD.** *Alas for that day! For the day of the LORD is near.* (Joel 1:13–15 NIV)

LET'S PRAY TOGETHER

God Almighty, in Jesus's precious name, we pray for mercy. We have sinned, and we have acted wickedly. Father, forgive us. Our generation has turned aside and pursued our own ways. Come, Lord, and forgive us of this sin. Come, Lord, and revive our hearts once again.

Come, Lord, and heal our land as we stand in the gap before You. Come, Lord Jesus, and reveal Your great mercy. Come, Lord, as we lay our hearts open before You. Come, Lord, because You alone have the answers for life's most desperate needs. In Jesus's mighty name, let revival breakthrough come. Let it be so. Amen and Amen!

PART TWO:

SACRIFICE RELEASES
SUPERNATURAL POWER

4

PRACTICAL ASPECTS OF FASTING

"Declare a holy fast; call a sacred assembly.
Summon the elders and all who live in the land to the house of the
LORD your God, and cry out to the LORD."
—Joel 1:14 (NIV)

The first three chapters of this book focused on prayer. In these next three chapters, we will examine the practical aspects of fasting, fasting for crisis intervention, and how fasting releases God's supernatural presence and power for revival breakthrough.

Some people are well-seasoned in the spiritual dimensions of revival, prayer, fasting, spiritual warfare, and the like, and some are not. Even if you are familiar with fasting, I ask that you push familiarity aside as you read this chapter, because familiarity can be a hindrance to a fresh approach to the Word of God, a hindrance to fresh revelation, and even a hindrance to new purposes of God. I believe God wants to give you fresh revelation today so that you can enter into a breakthrough leading to revival. Let us pray to that purpose:

Father, thank You for such a time as this. Again, we're asking for revelation—that You would show us how every prayer counts and every sacrifice matters. Please illuminate Your Word and inspire us to do our part in Your purposes, realizing that our participation really does matter. In Jesus's name, Amen and Amen.

WHAT IS FASTING?

Fasting is a deliberate act of turning away from food and/or other personal appetites for spiritual purposes, especially so that we can focus our attention on God. That is a very simple definition for a multifaceted topic. In this chapter, we will look at a number of those facets, including the following themes, as we examine this truly fascinating subject:

+ The nature of fasting
+ The purpose of fasting
+ Fasting for victory over Satan
+ Fasting in the Old and New Testaments
+ Fasting in the lives of church leaders in history
+ When to fast
+ Different types of fasts
+ How to fast: the ABCs of fasting
+ Physical realities of fasting
+ Suggestions for maximum physical benefits while fasting
+ Breaking a fast

THE NATURE OF FASTING

Sacrifice releases power, or a display of God's blessing. There is not a particular Bible verse that outright states, "Sacrifice releases power"; rather, it is a principle that it taught throughout both the Old and New Testaments. I personally consider periodic fasting essential, but not necessarily always in its purest form of abstaining from food. Fasting can also include choosing to forgo, for example, complaining, gossip, social media, or another negative trait or distraction. I have gone on a fast from negativity, which, take it from me, can be harder than fasting from food. I believe that fasting from whatever is a hindrance in your life is a sacrifice before God for spiritual benefit.[27]

In whatever form it takes, fasting enables us to consecrate ourselves to God at a higher level and to focus on Him with greater attention. Many believers don't understand or practice the Christian discipline of fasting. However, when we understand the purpose behind the task, it makes more sense, doesn't it?

THE PURPOSE OF FASTING

Fasting is designed to discipline the body and quiet the soul so that we can hear more clearly from God. The Scriptures show us that prayer and fasting are linked together. Fasting does not "buy" us anything from God; rather, it aligns us with His will, His Word, His purposes, and His ways.

When my book *The Lost Art of Practicing His Presence* was first published, I was sharing with someone how the book was a contemporary read on the spiritual disciplines. Immediately, I heard the Holy Spirit say something like, "Discipline, discipline. You don't have enough discipline to have a spiritual discipline." Although I firmly believed that I did indeed have discipline, I understood what the Holy Spirit was saying to me. He confirmed this when He added, "Disciplines are privileges—spiritual privileges." That idea shifted my mindset regarding how I presented these truths about spiritual disciplines. Fasting is a spiritual privilege. This act of discipline enables us to enter into the privilege of deeper intimacy with God. It's not about our working our way into His presence; it's all about His grace empowering us! Right?

Why is this understanding about fasting as a discipline important? Sometimes people can be so disciplined that their lives with God are like dried-up prunes! They don't have life; they have *religion*. To be disciplined does not always mean that we are full of life. We can be so disciplined that we're just religious twigs—all dried up, with no fruit!

God invites us into a spiritual partnership with Him. In conjunction with prayer, meditation on God's Word, and other righteous activities, fasting actually helps us to form this partnership with God.

---

27. For online classes on consecrated contemplative prayer, see godencounters.com.

FASTING FOR VICTORY OVER SATAN

One of the results of fasting is greater victory over Satan. In Mark 9, Jesus and three of His disciples, Peter, James, and John, witnessed the manifestation of all His glory on a mountain near Jerusalem. When they came down from the mountain, they found that the rest of the disciples had been attempting to deliver a boy who was demonized. They had frantically sought to gain a victory over the demon, but nothing seemed to bring deliverance.

Observing their difficulty, Jesus stepped forth and promptly healed the youth. Then the Master carefully instructed His disciples regarding the secret to the spiritual power, saying, *"This kind* [of demon] *can come out by nothing but prayer and fasting"* (Mark 9:29 NKJV).

This account in the gospel of Mark proves that fasting leads to direct power over darkness, over Satan. Whereas other types of prayer sometimes only slow Satan down, fasting *with prayer* stops Satan in his tracks. It is not that regular prayer is absent of power but that fasting with prayer is an amplification of that power. Isn't that awesome?

FASTING IN THE OLD AND NEW TESTAMENTS

There are numerous examples of both men and women in the Old and the New Testaments who fasted, including the following:

From the Old Testament:

+ Moses (See Exodus 34:28.)

+ Elijah (See 1 Kings 19:8.)

+ David (See 2 Samuel 12:16–17.)

+ Ezra (See Ezra 10:6.)

+ Daniel (See Daniel 10:3.)

+ Esther (See Esther 4:15–16.)

+ The nation of Israel (See, for example, Numbers 29:7 ["humbling themselves" implies fasting]; 1 Samuel 7:6; Nehemiah 9:1.)

From the New Testament:

+ Anna the prophetess (See Luke 2:36–37.)

+ Jesus (See Matthew 4:2; Luke 4:2.)

+ Paul (See Acts 9:9.)

+ Church leaders at Antioch (See Acts 13:2.)

+ Paul and Barnabas (See Acts 14:23.)

Here are several notable results of fasting and praying recorded in the Bible:

+ The Jews in exile were delivered from death. (See Esther 8–9.)

+ Daniel received divine instruction. (See Daniel 10.)

+ God's judgment on the entire city of Nineveh was reversed. (See Jonah 3–4.)

+ Demons were cast out. (See Mark 9:14–29 NKJV.)

+ The will of God was revealed. (See Acts 9:9–15; 13:1–4.)

+ Elders were chosen and ordained for the churches. (See Acts 14:23.)

These are just a few examples of how powerful prayer and fasting were—and are.

FASTING IN THE LIVES OF CHURCH LEADERS IN HISTORY

Fasting was vital not only in the lives of people in the Bible, but also in the lives of church leaders throughout history. Even a casual study of church history reveals how important fasting was to those who paved the way in spreading of the gospel around the world.

Martin Luther fasted regularly, as did John Knox. Christian leaders in later centuries also valued fasting. Consider the early days of the powerful Methodist Revival. John Wesley so believed in the importance of fasting that he refused to ordain young men to the ministry who would not fast two days each week. And Charles G. Finney wrote the following:

Sometimes I would find myself in a great measure empty of this power. I would go and visit, and find that I made no saving impression. I would exhort and pray with the same results. I would then set apart a day for private fasting and prayer, fearing that this power had departed from me, and would inquire anxiously after the reason of this apparent emptiness. After humbling myself and crying out for help, the power would return upon me with all its freshness. This has been the experience of my life.[28]

That is a leader of a revival and an awakening!

Here is an additional insight from Ole Hallesby, who played a leading role in the church's opposition to the Nazis, for which he was confined to a concentration camp for two years:

> To make use of a rather mechanical but nevertheless vivid illustration, we might compare this [fasting] with the transmission of electrical power. The greater the volume of power to be transmitted, the stronger the connection with the power house must be, that is, the larger the cable must be....
>
> Fasting helps to give us that inner sense of spiritual penetration by means of which we can discern clearly that for which the Spirit of prayer would have us pray in exceptionally difficult circumstances.[29]

Fasting creates a larger cable connection with the Powerhouse Power Source. Sounds right to me!

WHEN TO FAST

So, when do we fast? I offer the following times and circumstances when we should fast:

+ When the Holy Spirit leads us to do so

+ When we sense the need

+ When the church body is called to fast

+ When the national leadership calls a special time of fasting

---

28. Wesley L. Duewel, *Touch the World Through Prayer* (Grand Rapids, MI: Zondervan, 1986), 232.
29. Ole Hallesby, *Prayer* (Minneapolis, MN: Augsburg Fortress, 1994), 118. Hallesby (1879–1961) was a theologian, author, and educator.

♦   When we hear a heavenly "trumpet sound" calling a fast

Let's examine each of these reasons for fasting more closely.

WHEN THE SPIRIT LEADS

First, we fast when the Holy Spirit leads us to do so. Matthew 4:1–2 says, "*Then Jesus was led **by the Spirit** into the wilderness to be tempted by the devil. **After fasting** forty days and forty nights, he was hungry*" (NIV).

There is much fascinating truth in those two short sentences. I like to acknowledge that Jesus, as a human being, knew hunger. And, after forty days of not eating, it was only to be expected that He would be hungry. Yet I want you to know, as Jesus did, that, as you fast, the Holy Spirit can sustain you. As Jesus indicated in John 4:32 at a time when His disciples urged Him to eat physical food, there is "*food to eat that you do not know about*" until you get into the realms of fasting and are in living the midst of the will of the Father.

That's the truth. You'll lose your appetite for food, and your appetite for God will absolutely increase. Therefore, allow the Holy Spirit to lead you to fast, just as He led Jesus to fast.

WHEN WE SENSE THE NEED

Second, we fast when we sense a particular need for it. As a basis for this principle, let's read Matthew 6:16–18:

> **When you fast**, do not look somber as the hypocrites do, for they disfigure their faces to show others they are fasting. Truly I tell you, they have received their reward in full. But when you fast, put oil on your head and wash your face, so that it will not be obvious to others that you are fasting, but only to your Father, who is unseen; and your Father, who sees what is done in secret, will reward you.   (NIV)

As I emphasized above, this Scripture passage begins with the phrase "*When you fast.*" It doesn't say *if* you fast but *when* you fast, revealing that fasting was not just an Old Testament practice but was carried over into the New Testament. Followers of God in Jesus's day fasted as well; in fact, fasting was actually considered to be part of the consistent, regular pattern of a disciple's lifestyle. *"When you fast..."* is a statement of expectation, indicating, "You're going to fast, and here's the way to do it."

You may sense a need to fast during certain seasons of your life and/or according to a particular pattern each week or each month of the year.

WHEN THE CHURCH BODY IS CALLED TO FAST

Third, when the Holy Spirit calls the church as a body to fast, He presents a special, urgent need that requires community fasting and prayer.

It is safe to presume that you and I belong to different local church bodies. I'm part of a particular congregation in Nashville, and when that church calls a fast, I participate. For example, my church calls for a fast every fall that leads up to the new Hebrew year and the church's yearly fall conference. Likewise, you will follow your church's calls for fasts, knowing that the local leadership understands the needs of the people and feels that a special consecration and prayer emphasis is required.

Thus, we enter into fasts, in part, according to our alignment with particular believers and Christian leaders. That's a biblical concept. When we choose to be in this type of alignment, we are to follow our leaders. That is the way it should work. Your alignments will help you to determine when to fast.

WHEN THE NATIONAL LEADERSHIP CALLS A FAST

Fourth, there are also calls for fasts at the national level. When such an announcement is made, we need to tune our ears to hear that call. When the national leadership requests a special time of fasting, it is usually during a time of crisis. A biblical example of such a fast is Esther's call for a fast among all the Jews living in exile in Persia:

> *Then Esther sent this reply to Mordecai: "Go, **gather together** all the Jews who are in Susa, **and fast** for me. Do not eat or drink for three days, night or day. I and my attendants will fast as you do. When this is done, I will go to the king, even though it is against the law. And if I perish, I perish."* (Esther 4:15–16 NIV)

In the United States, each year, the first Thursday in May is set aside by presidential proclamation as the National Day of Prayer. That is one of the very first days that I mark on my calendar every year. No matter where I am in the world on that day, I participate in the National Day of Prayer. In fact, I request a role in helping to lead the National Day of Prayer, whether I'm in Nashville, New York City, Atlanta, or wherever. Ask my friends—I take that day seriously. In fact, I would like it to be called the National Day of Prayer *and Fasting*.

WHEN WE HEAR A HEAVENLY "TRUMPET SOUND"

The last aspect of when to fast belongs to a higher level: we fast when we hear a heavenly "trumpet sound":

Declare a holy fast; call a sacred assembly. Summon the elders and all who live in the land to the house of the LORD your God, and cry out to the LORD. (Joel 1:14 NIV)

Blow the trumpet in Zion, declare a holy fast, *call a sacred assembly.* **Gather the people,** *consecrate the assembly; bring together the elders, gather the children, those nursing at the breast. Let the bridegroom leave his room and the bride her chamber.* (Joel 2:15–16 NIV)

These verses express a special divine urgency to pray involving all the people of the land. Are you in tune to hear such a heavenly trumpet call? Is your heart aligned to follow the "trumpet in Zion"? Those are serious questions that each of us must answer.

To whose voice will you respond? Like you, I can't respond to every voice calling for a fast. We have to prioritize our efforts for maximum effort and effect. That's why relational alignment is so important. For example, if there is a national call for unity on the issue of abortion, that is serious, and I will participate. If Lou Engle or Cindy Jacobs or Ché Ahn calls for a fast, I will pay attention because I have relational equity with them and want to be supportive and aligned with them. Likewise, as I mentioned earlier, if the local church that I'm a part of calls for a fast, I'm definitely in on some level because I've already chosen to align with that body of believers. I urge you to listen to the voice of the Spirit regarding when to participate in the spiritual discipline and privilege of fasting.

I offer no condemnation for anyone who doesn't participate in fasting, but I hope you have learned how important this element is for revival breakthrough.

DIFFERENT TYPES OF FASTS

There are different types and variations of fasting.[30] Here, we will review the main forms of fasting: the regular fast; the partial fast; the liquid fast; and the absolute, or complete, fast. Yes, different leaders, denominations, and streams in the body of Christ might use slightly different terminology to describe the same concepts. So, let's be complementary and understanding, and move forward.

THE REGULAR FAST

A regular fast is when you refrain from eating all food and drink, except for water. This form of fasting might seem extreme to some who are just beginning to fast, but, historically, it has been a tool often used in the Master's hand. Most of the fasts I reference are of this nature. Along the way, I will point out a couple of exceptions from the Word of God. Note also that a regular fast is not a juice fast. And it is not the same as the Islamic tradition of a forty-day Ramadan fast in which people abstain from eating or drinking during daylight hours.

THE PARTIAL FAST

A partial fast is when you refrain from eating a certain meal or when you restrict the intake of certain foods. This type of fasting is often referred to as a "Daniel fast" because Daniel engaged in a type of fast in which he ate only vegetables. (See Daniel 10:3.) However, for some people, vegetarians and vegans, for example, a partial fast of vegetables would not really be a

---

30. I have taught extensively on the subject of fasting over the years, and I have included much of that teaching in this book. Other resources are my books *The Lost Art of Practicing His Presence* and *Prayer Storm: The Hour That Changes the World* (Shippensburg, PA: Destiny Image, 2013; soon to be rereleased as *Global Prayer Storm*). These books also include teachings on crisis intervention, the fasted life, and soaking in God's presence. At godencounters.com, I also offer an online class entitled "Prayer Storm."

fast at all because that is already their daily regimen and part of their lifestyle. Therefore, what is a fast to one person may not be a fast to another. In this regard, each person should fast according to their particular life situation.

I personally practice a dimension of intermittent fasting as a lifestyle, which involves abstaining from food for at least fourteen hours every day. Therefore, I don't necessarily consider that full fasting but rather partial fasting. I'm holding off on eating food for a period of time for purposes of rest, but I'm not necessarily doing it as a spiritual discipline. Rather, I do it as a focus unto the Lord, much as I might choose not to watch entertainment or read a book for pleasure in order to devote time to prayer and worship. See the difference?

When deciding which fast you want to try, pray about it and then obey as the Lord directs. For beginners and people with health restrictions, I have a word for you: if you can't do a complete, regular fast because of the requirements of certain medications you are taking or because of other health issues, don't. *There is no shame in that.* Some medications specifically state that they should be taken with food to alleviate side effects.

Also, some people suffer from nutritional deficiencies, which may be exacerbated during fasting. Diabetics must also be careful. Always be wise, but also consider the spiritual benefits of fasting. Many people need to enter into this form of focusing on God.

THE LIQUID FAST

A liquid fast involves not eating solid food for a predetermined period of time but allowing for the intake of liquids, such as broth, juices, and water. People who do extended fasts will use this form, even adding nutritional supplements to help sustain them over a long period. Again, be wise. Do not get hyper-spiritual! You must take care of yourself!

THE ABSOLUTE, TOTAL, OR COMPLETE FAST

The absolute or complete fast is often referred to as the "Esther fast." To go on a complete fast is to totally refrain from eating all food and drinking all liquid for a short, predetermined period of time. (See, for example, Esther 4:16; Acts 9:9.) Know that the average human body cannot survive without water for more than three days. This type of fast should only be entered into by the Lord's direct leading and the confirmation of others. But, as so, do what the Lord says. I have undergone Esther fasts in the past.

Yes, these fasts can be difficult and a great sacrifice—but they can also release incredible divine intervention. Remember the spiritual principle: sacrifice releases power.

THE ABCS OF FASTING

Now let's get practical about the manner in which we should fast. The following are some essential points to keep in mind.

IN SECRET

According to Matthew 6:18, we should fast in secret, *"so that your fasting will not be noticed by people but by your Father who is in secret; and your Father who sees what is done in secret will reward you."* But how can a fast be done in secret if it's a public fast? I encourage you to build a private history of fasting before God, not just a public history of fasting with other people. That's the goal.

Again, certain fasts will be called for on a national level and on the local church level. Additionally, when you fast, your family will be aware of what you're doing. What Jesus says in Matthew 6 about fasting in secret does not disqualify your fast if your fasting is known. Instead, it's about humbly and righteously obeying God—not projecting any self-righteousness. Jesus is really is talking about your heart attitude.

In line with this, according to Matthew 6:16–17, we should not fast with a sad countenance: *"Now whenever you fast, do not make a gloomy face as the hypocrites do, for they distort their faces so that they will be noticed by people when they are fasting. Truly I say to you, they have their reward in full. But as for you, when you fast, anoint your head and wash your face."* Fasting is a form of mourning. You're bringing a personal or corporate need before the Lord, or identifying with the needs of other people. But you do not draw unneeded attention to yourself.

WITH HUMILITY

According to Psalm 35:13, we should humble ourselves when fasting: "*I humbled my soul with fasting.*" Psalm 69:10 says, "*When I wept in my soul with fasting, it became my disgrace.*" Those who humble themselves before God receive grace from His throne. This is key to our understanding of the spiritual results of fasting. First Peter 5:6 says, "*Humble yourselves under the mighty hand of God, so that He may exalt you at the proper time.*"

Fasting is a tool that brings our soul under subjection to our heart-spirit, which is in union with Christ's Spirit. We are humbling our will, our mind, and our emotions—bringing them into subjection to God's rule and reign, into alignment with His will. In this way, we are posturing ourselves to receive more grace.

WITH PURE MOTIVES AND A PROPER ATTITUDE

In accordance with a humble spirit, we should fast with a pure motives and a proper attitude. When we read and study Isaiah 58:1–12, we see that fasting is not religious self-righteousness. Such "fasting" will get you nowhere. Rather, when you fast, seek the Lord with clean hands and a pure heart. "*Who may ascend the mountain of the LORD? Who may stand in his holy place? The one who has clean hands and a pure heart, who does not trust in an idol or swear by a false god. They will receive blessing from the LORD and vindication from God their Savior*" (Psalm 24:3–5 NIV).

What is the proper mindset for fasting? It is a *positive, faith-filled attitude of expectation.* It is God's will for us to fast, as stated in His Word. Therefore, we must believe that He will reward us when we fast according to the principles and instructions He has given us. (See, for example, Matthew 6:17–18; Hebrews 11:6.)

WITH THE RIGHT PERSPECTIVE TOWARD OUR BODIES

We should also fast with the right perspective toward our bodies. The human body is the temple of the Holy Spirit: "*Do you not know that your bodies are temples of the Holy Spirit, who is in you, whom you have received from God? You are not your own; you were bought at a price. Therefore honor God with your bodies*" (1 Corinthians 6:19–20 NIV). Our bodies are meant for God's use: *"Do not offer any part of yourself to sin as an instrument of wickedness, but rather offer yourselves to God as those who have been brought from death to life; and offer every part of yourself to him as an instrument of righteousness"* (Romans 6:13 NIV).

Fasting can make and keep our bodies strong and healthy. Friend, there are health benefits of fasting. This practice detoxes our bodies and can be used to help heal our bodies as well. Intermittent fasting calms our bodily functions and brings shalom, or rest, so that our bodies are not working all the time. We allow them to rest. Fasting can also actually be a healthy cleanse for our emotions as we spend less screen time with television, the Internet, smartphones, and so forth, and spend more time meditating on the Word and worshipping the Lord.

WITH BIBLE READING AND PRAYER

During a fast, I highly recommend that you take extra time for Bible reading and prayer. Also, guard against spiritual attack. Avoid religious ostentation and self-righteousness. (See Matthew 6:16–18.) When doing a group fast, all those involved should pray together, repent, confess sins, exercise faith, wait on God, and worship, worship, worship.

IN A PRACTICAL AND REALISTIC WAY

When fasting, be practical and realistic. Don't begin with a long fast. Instead, work up to it, cutting back on the last meal or two of the day. Consult a doctor if you have special health concerns. Your mental and spiritual attitudes are probably the most important aspects regarding fasting.

PHYSICAL REALITIES OF FASTING

When I started fasting, I didn't know that there would be some temporary adverse physical reactions. I just saw in the Bible that people fasted, so I thought I would too. I didn't realize that, about day three or four, I'd be walking through a brain fog. This symptom was actually part of the detox. Also, when a busting headache came along about the same time, I didn't realize it was related to caffeine withdrawal from my not drinking my regular tea. That's all it was. So, we must be aware of the physical realties of fasting and what to expect during the process.

In the early stages, unpleasant physical reactions may occur, especially when you are on an extended fast. If you regularly drink coffee, tea, caffeinated soda, or liquids of that nature, after about day two or three, or even later, you may experience headaches such as I did. However, a reaction might not be just caffeine withdrawal; your body might be craving something else. It may start to react to whatever you are denying it. Again, if you are taking medications, you have to be careful.

During this time, you might think, "Ugh, I can't handle this." I encourage you to push through it. This is when a right attitude about your body is essential. If you stand strong, you can press through the fog into mental clarity and get into a place of brightness—even better than before. You can do it!

During my beginning fast, I started feeling weak around day seven or so. I was tired physically on top of being hungry. I was ready for a Big Mac just for fortification. Even though I previously didn't even like Big Macs, I was ready for one! That's why it is called a "Big Mac attack," I guess!

Will your body get weak during a fast? Yes. You may even have to allow time to lie down for five minutes or so at various points throughout the day. You may have to walk a little more slowly. It's just basic physiology: when you aren't feeding your body as you normally would, your body will make adjustments. You may also experience low blood pressure and occasional lightheadedness, but these symptoms will go away as your body adjusts.

My friend Lou Engle used to humorously say, "I'm going down in history as the man who broke more fasts than I finished." Now, in reality, he and Mahesh Chavda have probably completed more fasts than anyone I know! Lou would get the munchies, stop and get a burger, and then repent. But again, Lou fasted more than anyone I know—he was committed to both the spiritual and physical benefits of fasting.

Other unpleasant physical reactions may include nausea. If you experience nausea, you probably need to back off from your fasting plan. Let me repeat: please be wise and take care of yourself. You may become dehydrated, which is common. Pay attention to what your body is telling you. Consult a physician if you have any concerns.

I used to suffer from hypoglycemia, and whenever I would try to do a forty-day fast, it was not good for me. I could do twenty-one days, but if I tried to go past that time frame, it was not healthy for me, and it was not good for my family.

However, for most of these issues, where temporary symptoms occur, don't stop your fast; rather, set your face to seek God's face. Keep in mind that you might need to alter your fasting plan along the way. Again, if reactions become severe, lie down and rest. And remember, if reactions become too severe, you may need to break your fast. If this happens, *do not condemn yourself.* Instead, learn from what happened. Maybe you need to cut back to fasting for only three days, which may be your limit, or perhaps you can build up to a longer fast.

SUGGESTIONS FOR MAXIMUM PHYSICAL BENEFITS WHILE FASTING

My suggestions for achieving the maximum physical benefits during a fast include making provision for resting, engaging in exercise, and getting some fresh air. Strength often increases about day five. It is wise to drink plenty of fluids—pure water or water with honey and lemon. The Bible talks about honey so much because it has various health benefits. Other good choices for liquids are fruit juices, broth, and Gatorade. However, caffeinated tea, coffee, or other such stimulants are not good for you during a fast.

Years ago, when I was fasting a lot, the Holy Spirit actually said to me, "You need to be careful. Your electrolytes are out of balance." Back then, I didn't even know what an electrolyte was, so I leaned in and I asked, "My what?" He said, "Your electrolytes are out of balance. Drink some Gatorade." Do you realize how practical a recommendation that was? The Holy Spirit told me on about day twenty-eight of a fast that I should be careful and drink Gatorade. That's how practical and personal God can be.

And, in case you're wondering, don't worry if your bowels don't move when you are on an extended fast. Things inside will temporarily shut down, but that doesn't mean you have a problem. There's just nothing in there to move. You'll be all right, and things will return to normal once you come off the fast. Again, if you have a concern, always consult your doctor.

BREAKING A FAST

When ending a fast, *always begin with a light meal*. The longer the fast, the more gradually you should break it. Your stomach will have contracted. Don't overexpand it by going to an all-you-can-eat buffet the first time. If you do, you will be in agony the next day. Believe me, I know. Also at the end of a fast, your body may still need extra rest.

The best advice for extended fasting is to begin the fast gradually and then break the fast gradually. That way you will benefit from a maximum, overall healthy, and good approach to fasting.

SET APART FOR GOD'S WORK

> *Now there were prophets and teachers at Antioch, in the church that was there: Barnabas, Simeon who was called Niger, Lucius of Cyrene, Manaen who had been brought up with Herod the tetrarch, and Saul. While they were **serving** [**performing ministry to or "worshiping,"** NIV, NLT] the Lord and fasting, the Holy Spirit said, "Set Barnabas and Saul apart for Me for the work to which I have called them." **Then, when they had fasted, prayed, and laid their hands on them, they sent them away.*** (Acts 13:1–3)

In Antioch, the leaders' fasting and prayers were received by the Lord as ministering unto Him and were used as tools to commission people into their callings. I fast and pray for the same for you, friend. May you be set apart for the work God has called you to perform.

LET'S PRAY TOGETHER

Father God, we desire that the Holy Spirit would teach us more of both the spiritual and the practical dimensions of fasting. Give us a revelation from the Word of God about the purpose of fasting as it pertains to revival breakthrough. Help us to avoid performance-based acceptance, a religious spirit, and self-righteousness. We believe that sacrifice releases power, and we volunteer freely to do our part because we believe that fasting is a spiritual privilege. It is an invitation to partner with You. In Jesus's mighty name, Amen and Amen.

5

FASTING FOR CRISIS INTERVENTION

"However, this kind does not go out except by prayer and fasting."
—Matthew 17:21 (NKJV)

The topic of fasting for crisis intervention is tremendously relevant in this time of political, economic, and spiritual turmoil in the nations of the world. Today, we are contending for personal breakthroughs, and we're contending for family breakthroughs. We're contending for breakthroughs on behalf of our churches, ministries, schools, and cities.

If we ever needed breakthroughs, we need them now because we are at a crossroads in history. But we have this opportunity: God invites us to be participants in making history before His throne. I believe that. Do you?

As we prepare to explore this essential topic, let's pray together:

Father, You are good, and Your mercies endure forever. We come before You in the name of Jesus, asking that You remove any blinders from our eyes so that we can discern what You would have us to see. We ask that where we are weary because we have already put our hand to this plow many times, You would invigorate us through the Holy Spirit. When You present us with another task or opportunity, renew us and give us Your vision. Help us to fulfill our roles as You carry out Your purposes in the world. In Jesus's name, Amen and Amen.

FOUR CRISES AND THEIR OUTCOMES

In this chapter, we will look at four Old Testament examples of how extreme crises were addressed or needs were met when people sought the Lord with fasting and prayer, prompting God's intervention and presence in those situations. When people react to major crises by the power of unified fasting, worship, praise, and prayer, God's remedy comes forth.

CRISIS 1: JEHOSHAPHAT AND THE ISRAELITES ATTACKED BY AN ENEMY ARMY

The first Old Testament example is the remarkable story from 2 Chronicles 20 about Jehoshaphat and the national fast in Israel during his reign. We will take a close look at how God responded to the people's earnest obedience at the looming crisis. This passage is rather lengthy, but it is an intriguing account and worth reading all the way through.

> After this, the Moabites and Ammonites with some of the Meunites came to wage war against Jehoshaphat.
>
> Some people came and told Jehoshaphat, "A vast army is coming against you from Edom, from the other side of the Dead Sea. It is already in Hazezon Tamar" (that is, En Gedi). **Alarmed, Jehoshaphat resolved to inquire of the LORD, and he proclaimed a fast for all Judah. The people of Judah came together to seek help from the LORD;** indeed, they came from every town in Judah to seek him.
>
> Then Jehoshaphat stood up in the assembly of Judah and Jerusalem at the temple of the LORD in the front of the new courtyard and said:
>
>> "LORD, the God of our ancestors, are you not the God who is in heaven? You rule over all the kingdoms of the nations. Power and might are in your hand, and no one can withstand you. Our God, did you not drive out the inhabitants of this land before your people Israel and give it forever to the descendants of Abraham your friend? They have lived in it and have built in it a sanctuary for your Name, saying, 'If calamity comes upon us, whether the sword of judgment, or plague or famine, we will stand in your presence before this temple that bears your Name and will cry out to you in our distress, and you will hear us and save us.'

*"But now here are men from Ammon, Moab and Mount Seir, whose territory you would not allow Israel to invade when they came from Egypt; so they turned away from them and did not destroy them. See how they are repaying us by coming to drive us out of the possession you gave us as an inheritance. Our God, will you not judge them? For we have no power to face this vast army that is attacking us. **We do not know what to do, but our eyes are on you.***"

All the men of Judah, with their wives and children and little ones, stood there before the LORD.

Then the Spirit of the LORD came on Jahaziel son of Zechariah, the son of Benaiah, the son of Jeiel, the son of Mattaniah, a Levite and descendant of Asaph, as he stood in the assembly.

He said: "Listen, King Jehoshaphat and all who live in Judah and Jerusalem! This is what the LORD says to you: 'Do not be afraid or discouraged because of this vast army. For the battle is not yours, but God's. Tomorrow march down against them. They will be climbing up by the Pass of Ziz, and you will find them at the end of the gorge in the Desert of Jeruel. You will not have to fight this battle. Take up your positions; stand firm and see the deliverance the Lord will give you, Judah and Jerusalem. **Do not be afraid; do not be discouraged. Go out to face them tomorrow, and the LORD will be with you.**'"

Jehoshaphat bowed down with his face to the ground, and **all the people of Judah and Jerusalem fell down in worship before the LORD.** Then some Levites from the Kohathites and Korahites stood up and **praised the LORD, the God of Israel**, with a very loud voice.

Early in the morning they left for the Desert of Tekoa. As they set out, Jehoshaphat stood and said, "Listen to me, Judah and people of Jerusalem! Have faith in the LORD your God and you will be upheld; have faith in his prophets and you will be successful." After consulting the people, Jehoshaphat appointed men to sing to the LORD and to praise him for the splendor of his holiness as they went out at the head of the army, saying:

"Give thanks to the LORD,
for his love endures forever."

As they began to sing and praise, the LORD set ambushes against the men of Ammon and Moab and Mount Seir who were invading Judah, *and they were defeated. The Ammonites and Moabites rose up against the men from Mount Seir to destroy and annihilate them. After they finished slaughtering the men from Seir, they helped to destroy one another.*

When the men of Judah came to the place that overlooks the desert and looked toward the vast army, they saw only dead bodies lying on the ground; no one had escaped. So Jehoshaphat and his men went to carry off their plunder, and they found among them a great amount of equipment and clothing and also articles of value—more than they could take away. There was so much plunder that it took three days to collect it. On the fourth day they assembled in the Valley of Berakah, where they praised the LORD. This is why it is called the Valley of Berakah to this day.

*Then, led by Jehoshaphat, all the men of Judah and Jerusalem **returned joyfully to Jerusalem, for the LORD had given them cause to rejoice over their enemies.** They entered Jerusalem and went to the temple of the LORD with harps and lyres and trumpets.*

*The fear of God came on all the surrounding kingdoms when they heard how the LORD had fought against the enemies of Israel. **And the kingdom of Jehoshaphat was at peace, for his God had given him rest on every side.*** (2 Chronicles 20:1–30 NIV)

In this passage, the significance and the value of Jehoshaphat's call for a national fast should not be overlooked. Important portions have been bolded for your attention. To summarize this thrilling episode in the chronicles of God's people: first, the crisis was acknowledged before the Lord; second, God provided a critical response. Here was the sequence of events:

- The people were called to unite in corporate fasting.
- The leader offered a sincere prayer of confession and dependence, appealing for mercy.
- God intervened and gave direction for action.
- The people responded with obedience and praise.
- God's presence was released, and victory was won.

This story reminds me of all the national fasts I've been participated in over the years. These were amazing gatherings, especially the ones held in Washington, DC. In 2001, I helped Lou Engle with The Call, a time of repentance and prayer for the United States, and I have participated in events celebrating the founding of America. I have also joined in fasts in many other countries.

I was recently pondering upon a dream I had in which I relived an actual occurrence when I took my mother to Washington, DC, in 1980 for a Washington for Jesus event that included a day of fasting. We traveled by bus together from Kansas City to the nation's capital. By accompanying my mother on this trip, I was helping her to fulfill a heartfelt desire. I had totally forgotten that I'd had the honor of going with my dear, praying mom to Washington, DC.

During my dream, I felt that the Lord was just letting me know that this trip had mattered and our presence at the event had helped. I think heaven was letting me know not only how much the trip meant to my mother, but also how much it meant to God. Prayer memories etched in the banks of heavenly accounts! So kind of God!

In the same way, God wants you to understand that He remembers your sacrifices—both your big efforts and your small efforts to obey Him. No matter how small, your sacrifices matter; every little act of obedience matters. They all make a difference to the Lord.

God remembers when Jehoshaphat called all the people of Judah to fast and how the people praised and worshipped Him. God commemorated that event by having it recorded in His book—the Bible, the book of remembrance. God recalls every act of worship. So, know that God remembers your sacrifices for revival breakthrough for your family; those sacrifices are written down in His book in heaven.

Likewise, God remembers our united corporate fasting, and He remembers our prayers of confession and dependence and mercy. At such times, He gives us direction, and our response should be one of extravagant praise, which releases God's presence in our midst.

CRISIS 2: EZRA AND THE EXILES FACE A PERILOUS JOURNEY

The eighth chapter of Ezra records God's intervention when a group of Jews living in Persia traveled back to Jerusalem after decades in exile. It was a long journey filled with many possible dangers. The group included women and children, all the people's possessions, and sacred temple vessels. Rather than ask the authorities for soldiers to accompany them, Ezra and the rest of the exiles chose to fast and seek God for a safe journey:

> Then **I proclaimed a fast** there at the river of Ahava, to humble ourselves before our God, **to seek from Him a safe journey** for us, our little ones, and all our possessions. For I was ashamed to request from the king troops and horsemen to protect us from the enemy on the way, because we had said to the king, "The hand of our God is favorably disposed to all who seek Him, but His power and His anger are against all those who abandon Him." **So we fasted and sought our God** concerning this matter, **and He listened to our pleading.** (Ezra 8:21–23)

The people chose God's supernatural protection, and the result was that they completed the long journey in perfect peace and safety.

> Then we journeyed from the river Ahava on the twelfth of the first month to go to Jerusalem; and **the hand of our God was upon us, and He rescued us from the hand of the enemy and the ambushes by the road.** So we came to Jerusalem and remained there for three days.... The exiles who had come from the captivity **offered burnt offerings to the God of Israel.** (Ezra 8:31–32, 35)

God remembered the crisis that Ezra and the exiles faced and how they responded to it. He included an account of it in His Word so that, many centuries later, we could glean from it the wisdom of engaging in fasting and prayer during difficult and frightening times.

CRISIS 3: ESTHER AND THE JEWS THREATENED WITH EXTINCTION

As we noted in the previous chapter, Esther's call for a fast caused God to intervene and save all of the Jewish people in the Persian Empire from extinction. Behind the scenes, the evil Haman, a high official of the emperor Ahasuerus (also known as Xerxes), was influenced by unseen spiritual forces to plot the extermination of the Jews. This was not merely flesh versus flesh; it was spirit versus Spirit.

The first chapter of Esther details the lavish banquet King Ahasuerus held for all his dignitaries. When Queen Vashti refused to appear at the king's request, Ahasuerus took steps to replace her. Chapter 2 tells us about

Hadassah, a beautiful young Jewess, and her older cousin, Mordecai, a lower official in the empire who had raised her. Hadassah, renamed Esther, gained favor with the king, and Ahasuerus made her his new queen. In an intriguing turn of events, Mordecai discovered an assassination plot against the king, saving the king's life.

Esther 3 details Haman's anger against Mordecai for not bowing down to him. When Haman learned that Mordecai was a Jew, he extended his anger toward all the Jews throughout the kingdom, and he devised a plan to have them annihilated by the king's order. (Ahasuerus was unaware that Esther was a Jewess.) In chapter 4, Mordecai told Esther about Haman's plot, urging her to intervene, and Esther devised a plan to save her people.

> *Then Esther told them to reply to Mordecai, "Go, **gather all the Jews who are found in Susa, and fast** for me; do not eat or drink for three days, night or day. **I and my attendants also will fast in the same way.** And then I will go in to the king, which is not in accordance with the law; and if I perish, I perish." So Mordecai went away and did just as Esther had commanded him.* (Esther 4:15–17)

Chapters 5 and 6 reveal Esther's elaborate plan. In the remaining chapters, Haman was hanged on the very gallows where he conspired to have Mordecai meet his final demise, Mordecai was promoted to a high position by the king, the Jews destroyed their enemies, and the Feast of Purim was instituted. Thus, in God's plan, Esther and Mordecai were promoted to the two most influential positions in the Persian Empire, after the king. The entire book of Esther is fascinating, and I encourage you to take the time to read and study it.

What was the result of God's intervention in response to the people's fasting and prayers? It was the saving of His people from total destruction.

CRISIS 4: A CITY ON THE VERGE OF JUDGMENT

To me, God's intervention in Nineveh is one of the most outrageous and remarkable testimonies in the entire Bible. The story begins with God's command to His prophet Jonah, and Jonah's disobedience:

The word of the L*ORD* *came to Jonah the son of Amittai, saying,* *"Arise, go to Nineveh, the great city, and cry out against it, because* *their wickedness has come up before Me." But Jonah got up to flee to* *Tarshish from the presence of the* L*ORD. So he went down to Joppa,* *found a ship that was going to Tarshish, paid the fare, and boarded it* *to go with them to Tarshish away from the presence of the* L*ORD.*

(Jonah 1:1–3)

Destruction was about to come upon the city of Nineveh because of the people's wickedness. But God, in His abundant mercy, wanted to warn the Ninevites, through Jonah, to repent and be spared. Jonah would have rather seen the Ninevites destroyed, so he fled from the assignment—and the Lord. Jonah soon found himself in the middle of the sea within the belly of a giant fish. Eventually, he acknowledged the Lord and called upon Him, and God delivered him from his predicament. Jonah finally obeyed God and went to Nineveh, declaring to the people, *"Forty more days, and Nineveh will be overthrown"* (Jonah 3:4).

Then the people of Nineveh believed in God; and they called a fast *and put on sackcloth, from the greatest to the least of them. When the* *word reached the king of Nineveh, he got up from his throne, removed* *his robe from himself, covered himself with sackcloth, and sat on the* *dust. And he issued a proclamation, and it said, "In Nineveh by the* *decree of the king and his nobles: No person, animal, herd, or flock* *is to taste anything. They are not to eat, or drink water. But every* *person and animal must be covered with sackcloth; and people are to* *call on God vehemently, and they are to turn, each one from his evil* *way, and from the violence which is in their hands. Who knows, God* *may turn and relent, and turn from His burning anger so that we will* *not perish." When God saw their deeds, that they turned from their* *evil way, then God relented of the disaster which He had declared He* *would bring on them. So He did not do it.* (Jonah 3:5–10)

This was a historic national repentance, and God heard and responded with mercy. Does that give you encouragement? It does for me. Is there discipline, is there sacrifice, in fasting? Yes! Is there privilege, is there reward, in fasting? Yes!

BLESSINGS FROM FASTING

The following passage from Isaiah 58 presents many of the blessings we will receive by choosing to fast as we endeavor to obey the Lord and serve others on His behalf. Again, fasting is more than just abstaining from food; it is realigning our lives with God's heart, will, and purposes in our generation.

> *Is not this the kind of fasting I have chosen: to loose the chains of injustice and untie the cords of the yoke, to set the oppressed free and break every yoke? Is it not to share your food with the hungry and to provide the poor wanderer with shelter—when you see the naked, to clothe them, and not to turn away from your own flesh and blood? Then your light will break forth like the dawn, and your healing will quickly appear; then your righteousness will go before you, and the glory of the LORD will be your rear guard. Then you will call, and the LORD will answer; you will cry for help, and he will say: Here am I. If you do away with the yoke of oppression, with the pointing finger and malicious talk, and if you spend yourselves in behalf of the hungry and satisfy the needs of the oppressed, then your light will rise in the darkness, and your night will become like the noonday. The LORD will guide you always; he will satisfy your needs in a sun-scorched land and will strengthen your frame. You will be like a well-watered garden, like a spring whose waters never fail. Your people will rebuild the ancient ruins and will raise up the age-old foundations; you will be called Repairer of Broken Walls, Restorer of Streets with Dwellings.* (Isaiah 58:6–12 NIV)

To summarize this passage from Isaiah, fasting with obedience…

+ loosens the chains of injustice.

+ sets the oppressed free.

+ breaks yokes of bondage.

+ promotes sharing.

+ provides for the needy.

+ brings healing.

+ springs forth righteousness.

+ brings God's glory to protect you.

+ assures that God will answer your calls for help.

+ encourages living righteously and being benevolent.

+ means the Lord will guide you and satisfy your needs.

+ strengthens your body.

+ causes you to be fruitful and productive.

+ can launch you into being a minister of reconciliation.

I have taught on crisis intervention quite a lot, and this topic can get very heavy at times. In my book *Prayer Storm* and its related teaching curriculum, I delve deeper into what really makes a difference and is an encouragement during difficult times. Fasting is a tool that gives believers in Christ Jesus manifest power over the works of darkness. The fasting principle we can stand on is this: *sacrifice releases greater power.*

GOD IS WILLING!

Ezekiel 36:37 tells us, *"This is what the* Lord *God says: 'This too I will let the house of Israel ask Me to do for them: I will increase their people like a flock.'"* The first time I spoke on this verse, I was part of the ministry team with Mike Bickle at Kansas City Fellowship. I was new to the staff, and, in those days, I referred to myself as a "treacher" because I wasn't a full-blown preacher and I wasn't really a full-blown teacher. At the end of the message, when I taught that God is willing to help us, the people gave a standing ovation.

Experiencing such a reaction has only happened to me three times in my entire life. I believe that, on that particular day, it was a sign from heaven of favor that I was at the right place at the right time. God does help weak people, and He does bring confirmation! But the fact that God is willing to act on our behalf is a powerful message, and it drew forth that kind of response from the people.

My message based on Ezekiel 36:37 presented the following principle, which I expressed in chapter 3 of this book: "If we will, God will." The preamble of the principle is knowing for certain that God is able and willing. To get to revival breakthrough, we must have a renewed mindset of trusting that God is willing to help us—during great crises and in the everyday needs of life alike.

If your prayers are not based on knowing that God is willing, you may need to identify hindrances that are keeping you from trusting Him completely. You have to get to a place where you know that you know this truth: not only is God *capable*, not only is God *able*, but *God is also willing.* Then you can call forth God's intervention in every situation.

If you don't believe that He is willing, then what is the basis for His intervention? There is none.

The *New King James Version* translates Ezekiel 36:37 in this way: "*I will also **let** the house of Israel inquire of Me to do this for them.*" And look at the language used in the *New International Version* for this verse: "*This is what the Sovereign* LORD *says: Once again I will **yield** to Israel's plea and do this for them: I will make their people as numerous as sheep.*" God says, "*I will yield….*" He will concede or allow; in other words, He is inviting us into a partnership with Him.

Remember when we discussed how God never changes? Again, He never changes His character, but He does change His mind on occasion. He Himself often prompts us to request such intervention, as He did by warning the Ninevites of their impending destruction due to their wickedness.

This principle is so crucial that I want you to follow me closely now: *God will,* but He is waiting for you to recognize that He will so that you will ask Him to do what He said that He will. Do you get it? Slowly read this verse again:

> *This is what the Sovereign* LORD *says: Once again **I will yield to Israel's plea and do this for them**: I will make their people as numerous as sheep.* (Ezekiel 36:37 NIV)

If you will, God will—but you must *know* that God is willing. This principle is found in multiple places throughout God's Word. For example, remember that 2 Chronicles 7:14 says, "***If my people***, *who are called by my name, will humble themselves and pray and seek my face and turn from their wicked ways,* ***then I will*** *hear from heaven, and I will forgive their sin and* *will heal their land"* (NIV). And in Jeremiah 18:7–8, God tells us, *"At one moment I might speak concerning a nation or concerning a kingdom to uproot, to pull down, or to destroy it;* **if that nation** *against which I have spoken turns from its evil,* **I will relent....**" If God says He's going to, then God is going to.

Let's read more from the passage in Jeremiah 18:

> At one moment I might speak concerning a nation or concerning a kingdom to uproot it, to tear it down, or to destroy it; if that nation against which I have spoken turns from its evil, I will relent of the disaster that I planned to bring on it. Or at another moment I might speak concerning a nation or concerning a kingdom to build up or to plant it; if it does evil in My sight by not obeying My voice, then I will relent of the good with which I said that I would bless it.
>
> (Jeremiah 18:7–10)

During the eighth century BC, Israel, a nation with spiritual foundations, received warnings from four prophets—Amos, Hosea, Isaiah, and Micah—while Nineveh, an evil nation, received one warning from one prophet—Jonah. What was the outcome? Israel did not repent, and the Assyrian Empire became an instrument of judgment on them. In 721 BC, Assyria captured and destroyed Samaria, the capital of Israel at that time, and took the people into captivity.

On the other hand, the Ninevites repented when they heard God's warning and were spared His judgment at that time. We see that God is willing to intervene for us in times of crisis. He has given us the capacity to participate with Him in crisis intervention, which includes fasting.

One aspect of the nature or character of God is that He is an invitational, participatory God. He enjoys engaging with His children to fulfill His purposes. We must always remember that God invites us to co-labor with Him! He could do it all, but, in His sovereignty, He has chosen to invite us into His process of ruling and reigning with Him. He loves working with us!

As we consider crisis intervention, let us also remember that God is faithful all the time. God's mercy always triumphs over judgment. That is the nature of our Lord. Yet we must come to understand the various dimensions of God's nature to get as close to knowing Him as possible here on earth. And, as I have emphasized in this chapter, one of those dimensions is that not only is He able, not only is He capable, but He is also *willing.*

There was one day a year—only one—that was mandated under the old covenant when everyone would fast on a national level: the Day of Atonement. And there was one day a year when the high priest went beyond the veil into the manifest presence of God—that same day. Do you think there's a correlation? I will leave you with that thought now, but we will return to it later in this book.

I conclude this chapter with a special warning and encouragement from the late Derek Prince, a noted Bible teacher:

> Today, God is speaking once again through His messengers and by His Spirit to cities and to nations. He is calling to repentance, to fasting, to self-humbling. Those who obey will receive the visitation of His mercy, as Nineveh did. Those who reject will receive the visitation of His wrath, as Israel did.[31]

Let us beware that we do not allow our familiarity with the message to keep us from acknowledging its urgency. Let us be encouraged, as we remove the familiarity, so that we can respond in obedience to the Word, the will, and the ways of God, in Jesus's name.

LET'S PRAY TOGETHER

> Gracious heavenly Father, we look at the examples of crisis intervention through fasting in the lives of Jehoshaphat, Ezra, Esther, the Ninevites, and others, and we become inspired. We believe that what You did before, You want to do again. As we repent and fast, release the power of Your Spirit in an unprecedented revival. Send Your Spirit now more powerfully, for Jesus Christ's sake. In His name, Amen and Amen.

---

31. Derek Prince, *Shaping History Through Prayer and Fasting* (New Kensington, PA: Whitaker House, 2018), 128.

6

FASTING RELEASES GOD'S PRESENCE AND POWER

"Now in the church at Antioch there were prophets and teachers:
Barnabas, Simeon called Niger, Lucius of Cyrene, Manaen
*(who had been brought up with Herod the tetrarch) and Saul. **While***
***they were worshiping the Lord and fasting**, the Holy Spirit said,*
'Set apart for me Barnabas and Saul for the work to which I have
*called them.' So **after they had fasted and prayed**, they placed their*
hands on them and sent them off."
—Acts 13:1–3 (NIV)

Our theme verse for this chapter comes from one of my favorite portions of the entire Bible: Acts 13. Because I love this passage so much, I have intensely studied the first three verses. Verses 2 and 3 both mention fasting, and verse 3 also says that the group was praying. These leaders at Antioch came from diverse backgrounds, but they were all in one accord while they were *"worshiping the Lord and fasting."* Fasting was a dimension of their vertical ministry to God. Then, in the midst of this worship, *"the Holy Spirit said, 'Set apart for me Barnabas and Saul for the work to which I have called them.' So after they had fasted and prayed, they placed their hands on them and sent them off."*

In Acts 13:1, these leaders were identified as *"prophets and teachers."* Yet after the Holy Spirit spoke, Paul and Barnabas were known as "apostles." That's who "sent ones" are.

I want you to note the order of the words in verse 2. The Holy Spirit said, *"Set apart **for me** Barnabas and Saul...."* First the Spirit aligned Himself with the men; *"the work"* came next. For many of us, there is often a tension between our call and our work. We're all called to put our hand to the plow to do a really good work for the kingdom. And we all know that *"faith without works is dead"* (James 2:26). But we need to acknowledge the proper order of things. I believe that the Holy Spirit wanted these two men to be devoted to Him first and to the work second, which I call the "jealousy of God." In other words, to God, relationship is primary. Likewise, we are to set ourselves apart for God first; then He enables us, through His supernatural grace, presence, power, and gifting, to do whatever work He has called us to do.

We can't overemphasize this point: we are *first* to be devoted to God, and *then* we are to do our work. That is the proper order, and we need to maintain it in our lives. If we allow our work to become all-encompassing, God can become an afterthought for us. We must set ourselves apart for Him, keeping Him first in everything we do.

Let's ask God for His blessing on our lives and for the illumination of His Word as we progress through this chapter.

> Father, we thank You that sacrifice releases power. Yet, in Your mysterious, majestic will, Word, and ways, sacrifice also releases a realm of Your presence. We cannot earn the manifestation of Your presence. However, we align our lives with Your Word, and we know that You show up when we sincerely seek You—just as You did for the disciples in Antioch as recorded in Acts 13. We come to You on behalf of our families, our cities, and our nations because of the difficult days in which we are living. We want to align ourselves with You because we need more of Your presence and Your power in these times. Today, we long to hear Your voice say, "Set apart for Me [insert your name] for the work for which I've called this child of Mine." Amen and Amen!

JOEL'S LAST-DAYS CRY: DESOLATION, THEN RESTORATION

Fasting releases God's presence and power in times when we have a personal or corporate need, when we require direction for ministry, and even when we face national destruction. In this regard, we move from Acts 13 to the book of Joel, which presents a pattern from which we can learn much about fasting.

Joel speaks about the last-days outpouring, but it also paints for us an extremely vivid picture of desolation through the invasion of demons:

> What the locust swarm has left the great locusts have eaten; what the great locusts have left the young locusts have eaten; what the young locusts have left other locusts have eaten. Wake up, you drunkards, and weep! Wail, all you drinkers of wine; wail because of the new wine, for it has been snatched from your lips. A nation has invaded my land, a mighty army without number; it has the teeth of a lion, the fangs of a lioness. It has laid waste my vines and ruined my fig trees. It has stripped off their bark and thrown it away, leaving their branches white. (Joel 1:4–7 NIV)

What a description of desolation! What were once fruitful vines and trees are now stripped bare. Everything has been laid to waste. Thankfully, chapter 2 of Joel contains a beautiful story of restoration. I believe that five words define our calling today, and they all start with "re": repent, reset, recalibrate, recover, and restore—or, in its noun form, restoration. When we face dire times, we need to repent of our sins, reset our priorities, recalibrate our focus, recover our devotion to God, and experience His presence and power in restoration.

Let us now go to the second chapter of Joel, where God speaks about that restoration:

> I will repay you for the years the locusts have eaten—the great locust and the young locust, the other locusts and the locust swarm—my great army that I sent among you. You will have plenty to eat, until you are full, and you will praise the name of the LORD your God, who has worked wonders for you; never again will my people be shamed. Then you will know that I am in Israel, that I am the LORD your God, and

that there is no other; never again will my people be shamed.

(Joel 2:25–27 NIV)

We must ask the question, "How did they—and how do we—get from desolation to restoration?" The answer is in *consecration*. For an individual, a church, a ministry, a city, or a nation, the only way to get from desolation to the manifestation of the promised restoration is to cross the bridge of consecration. This means to set yourself apart for God and His will, committing your life and your time to Him.

Joel 1:14 says that the people were to "*declare a holy fast; call a sacred assembly. Summon the elders and all who live in the land to the house of the* LORD *your God, and cry out to the* LORD" (NIV). This verse comes before the verses about God restoring the land. The people were called to consecrate themselves, sanctify themselves, set themselves apart for the Lord. This is a special act of obedience that requires intentionality—a purposeful and focused act of repentance before God.

Thus, in the book of Joel, the Lord Himself reveals the answer to the question, "How do we go from desolation to restoration?" I encourage you to study this entire biblical book so you can fully understand the template of repentance and restoration that it reveals.

We look next at Joel 2:12–17 in a different Bible version. Note the various emphases:

That is why the LORD *says, "**Turn to me now**, while there is time. **Give me your hearts. Come with fasting, weeping, and mourning.** Don't tear your clothing in your grief, but tear your hearts instead." **Return to the** LORD *your God, for he is merciful and compassionate, slow to get angry and filled with unfailing love. **He is eager to relent** and not punish. Who knows? Perhaps he will give you a reprieve, sending you a blessing instead of this curse. Perhaps you will be able to **offer grain and wine to the** LORD *your God as before. Blow the ram's horn in Jerusalem! **Announce a time of fasting; call the people together for a solemn meeting.** Gather all the people—the elders, the children, and even the babies. Call the bridegroom from his quarters and the bride from her private room. **Let the priests**, who minister in the* LORD's *presence, **stand and weep** between the entry room to the Temple and* *the altar.* **Let them pray**, *"Spare your people, Lord! Don't let your special possession become an object of mockery. Don't let them become a joke for unbelieving foreigners who say, 'Has the God of Israel left them?'"* (NLT)

This passage shows us how we can move from private consecration into corporate revival, which can then turn into large-scale revival breakthrough for a city, state, or nation. It can become a public movement that touches multitudes for the Lord. Joel 2:15 says, *"Blow the ram's horn in Jerusalem! Announce a time of fasting; call the people together for a solemn meeting"* (NLT). This is a set of public proclamations and corporate involvement. Then, Joel 2:16 states, *"Gather all the people"* (NLT), and Joel 2:17 says, *"Let the priests... stand and weep.... Let them pray, 'Spare your people, Lord!'"* (NLT).

We previously discussed the times when we should fast, which include when called upon by the Holy Spirit, by the local church leadership, by personal alignments, and by national proclamations. All these instances are reflected in this passage in Joel. I believe we're in such a time right now. Trumpets calling for repentance and prayer are being sounded by many Christians—nationwide and worldwide.

In Joel 2:1, the priests led the people into repentance and prayer. In both the past and the present, many Christian leaders and ministries have organized gatherings to call believers to publicly declare God's sovereignty over cities, states, and nations. Whether it was Franklin Graham's Prayer March 2020, Jonathan Cahn's The Return, Lou Engle's The Call/The Contend, or Cindy Jacobs's Reformation Prayer Network, the Holy Spirit has been stirring hearts and minds to come together for solemn assemblies to repent, reset, recalibrate, recover, and experience restoration.

As I indicated earlier, I have been involved in many such events and gatherings. I can tell you for a fact that wherever you live in the world, if you spiritually tune in, you will hear the Holy Spirit giving this call to fasting and prayer. The angels of heaven are blowing trumpets right now for people to gather and declare God's sovereignty. Align yourself with the Lord and give yourself to Him in this season because it is a fresh season of consecration. This is a necessary preliminary season, and if we will, corporately as well as individually, give ourselves to the sound of the trumpet, we may make a difference that we could not make individually.

GOD'S PROMISE WHEN CONDITIONS ARE MET

In Joel 2:28, God declares, *"And **afterward, I will pour out my Spirit on all people**. Your sons and daughters will prophesy, your old men will dream dreams, your young men will see visions"* (NIV). What came *before* this promise from God to pour out His Spirit on all people? Solemn assemblies, prayer and fasting, seeking God's face. Again, there are conditions that need to be met in order to unlock our individual and corporate prophetic destinies.

Restoration comes as believers meet God's conditions. The Lord cherishes His people, and His Word says:

Then the LORD was jealous for his land and took pity on his people. The LORD replied to them: "I am sending you grain, new wine and olive oil, enough to satisfy you fully; never again will I make you an object of scorn to the nations."... Be glad, people of Zion, rejoice in the LORD your God, for he has given you the autumn rains because he is faithful. He sends you abundant showers, both autumn and spring rains, as before.
(Joel 2:18–19, 23 NIV)

Psalm 103:1–5 elaborates on our heavenly Father's love for us:

*Praise the LORD, my soul; all my inmost being, praise his holy name. Praise the LORD, my soul, and forget not all his benefits—who **forgives all your sins** and **heals all your diseases**, who **redeems your life** from the pit and **crowns you with love and compassion**, who **satisfies your desires with good things** so that your youth is renewed like the eagle's.*
(NIV)

The crucial word in Joel 2:28 is *"afterward." After* the people assemble, fast, and pray, there will be a divine outpouring of the Holy Spirit upon all peoples, with signs and wonders. A great cry for salvation will result.

And afterward, I will pour out my Spirit on all people. Your sons and daughters will prophesy, your old men will dream dreams, your young men will see visions. Even on my servants, both men and women, I will pour out my Spirit in those days. I will show wonders in the heavens and on the earth, blood and fire and billows of smoke. The sun will be turned to darkness and the moon to blood before the coming of the great and dreadful day of the LORD. And everyone who calls on the name of the LORD will be saved; for on Mount Zion and in Jerusalem there will be deliverance, as the LORD has said, even among the survivors whom the LORD calls. (Joel 2:28–32 NIV)

After we meet the conditions, God does what only God can do. We are given small keys to open big doors. Again, the basic premise of what we have been reviewing is that *sacrifice releases God's presence and power.* God is sovereign, and He can do everything and anything without us. Yet, in His sovereignty, He has chosen to invite us to be His co-laborers. He has chosen not to act without us, so He welcomes us as His partners. He happily provides us with keys to revival breakthrough. This is God's promise when the conditions are met.

A TYPE OF END-TIMES FULFILLMENT

For yet another perspective on how fasting releases God's presence and power, we look at the observance of the Day of Atonement as a type or shadow of end-times fulfillment. The Day of Atonement, also known as Yom Kippur, is detailed in Leviticus 16. Here are several significant verses from that chapter:

*This is to be a **lasting ordinance** for you: **On the tenth day of the seventh month you must deny yourselves and not do any work**— whether native-born or a foreigner residing among you—because **on this day atonement will be made for you, to cleanse you.** Then, before the LORD, you will be clean from all your sins. **It is a day of sabbath rest**, and **you must deny yourselves; it is a lasting ordinance.*** (Leviticus 16:29–31 NIV)

The Day of Atonement was to be a "*lasting ordinance.*" By emphasizing this point, am I—even in part—trying to put us, as New Testament believers, under the law? No, the Lamb of God has fulfilled everything that was needed for us to have a restored relationship with the Father. As Jesus the Messiah said on the cross, "*It is finished!*" (John 19:30). Jesus came to fulfill the law, not to abolish it. (See Matthew 5:17.) There's an important difference.

So, how are we to perceive the Day of Atonement? Remember, it is a shadow of the end-times fulfillment. In various translations, Leviticus 16:29 says that the prerequisite for the cleansing and forgiveness is to *"humble yourselves"* (NASB), *"deny yourselves"* (NIV), or *"afflict your souls"* (NKJV). An in-depth study of that phrase reveals that it is used synonymously with fasting. Studying the Bible deeply is like searching for gold. We find some nuggets lying on the surface, but others we need to dig for. To "afflict your soul" is another way of saying to humble yourself, and one way to humble yourself is through fasting.

In Acts 27:9, the Day of Atonement is called *"the fast."* So, we know that even in the early church, atonement fasting was recognized and observed. As noted earlier, there was actually only one day every year when the Jewish people were required to fast, and that was the Day of Atonement. This wasn't the *only* day they fasted, but it was the only day when they were all *required* to fast.

By the way, we also know that the early church had an *"hour of prayer"* (Acts 3:1), because the book of Acts says Peter and John went up together to the temple during that time. Thus, in the early church, the believers followed certain norms, and some of those norms were the observance of the Day of Atonement and the hour of prayer, as well as the major Jewish feasts. The Christian church has Jewish roots, and certain dimensions were simply carried over to it.

If we don't understand the church's Hebraic roots, we may be confused by some of these references. For more than three thousand years, the Jewish people have been observing Yom Kippur by fasting. I have been in Israel many times during the High Holy or High Holiday dates; and, on Yom Kippur in particular, the entire nation screeches to a halt. There is no air or bus transportation, and there are no cars on the roads. Businesses are closed, and even the radio and television stations are off the air. (I wish our nation would do the same!)

Some Christians observe the Day of Atonement every year, not from an obligation to the law but to honor God's specific ordinance. As I described earlier, I believe that spiritual disciplines are a privilege. To consecrate ourselves on holy days is a privilege, not an obligation. Friend, I'm not trying to send you on a guilt trip, saying that you must observe all the Jewish feasts.

Rather, I'm trying to enlighten you to a privilege. No matter where I am in the world, I always set apart the Day of Atonement as a day of humbling my soul before the Lord—again, not out of religious obligation but out of delight that I'm spending that extra time with my Maker and Master. And guess what? He always shows up!

I believe the Day of Atonement is a shadow of the reality that we have with the Lamb of God "beyond the veil," or in the heavenly realm. On the Day of Atonement, the Israelite high priest went through the second veil into the holy of holies. Similarly, collective fasting precedes accompanying our High Priest along the path into the Holy Place inside the veil. And, in the new covenant, believers are called a *"holy priesthood"* (1 Peter 2:5). As we, the body of Christ, collectively enter into the joy of humbling our souls by fasting, we experience a greater release of God's holy presence.

FASTING FOR REVIVAL BREAKTHROUGH

The book of Joel depicts the principle that fasting precipitates the latter rain of God's presence. Remember that *after these things, God will pour out His Spirit on all people.* When there is an increase in the various forms of fasting among the global body of Christ, we should expect an unprecedented outpouring of God's presence upon all humankind. *If we will, He will.* Remember that!

Therefore, the pattern is set before us: the people sacrificed by fasting; they worshipped and prayed; the priests entered into the sanctuary and wept and interceded, and God poured out His presence. If we want more of Him, let's follow the Old Testament pattern with New Testament grace. Then let's watch and experience God's glorious presence flood planet Earth. As explained earlier, this is a shadow of the old covenant, and we in the new covenant get to live out the reality of fasting for revival breakthrough!

The following are some events from church history that combined the sacrifice of fasting with great outpourings.

A lot has been written and talked about regarding the great healing movements of 1948 and following. But do you know what happened shortly before that time of healing? In 1946, Franklin Hall published a book entitled *Atomic Power with God, Thru Fasting and Prayer.* I actually own a copy.

The book, which provided detailed information on the methods and benefits of fasting, was an immediate success and brought Hall considerable fame. According to Hall, all of the major evangelists began following his fasting regime and miracles erupted everywhere. Many observers of the early revival years agreed, as one said, "Every one of these men down through the years followed Franklin Hall's method of fasting."[32]

This example shows us that we must not only look at the fruit of healing movements but at their root systems as well. It is as we just discussed: "*Afterward....*" (Joel 2:28 NIV) comes the restoration.

A leader who has impacted my life in the area of fasting, as well as in other spiritual arenas, is Mahesh Chavda, senior pastor of All Nations Church in the Charlotte area of North Carolina. For decades, his ministry has been engaged in two forty-day fasts each year. He has seen hundreds of thousands come to faith in the Lord Jesus Christ, as well as every type of healing listed in the New Testament, including the raising of the dead; people healed of deafness, blindness, and AIDS; people delivered from curses; and many other miracles. Mahesh says, "The praying believer is the confident believer. But the fasting believer is the overcoming believer. This is the believer who changes the circumstances and the world around him."[33]

I mentioned earlier that many Christian leaders from the past and the present have called for corporate prayer. One example is Campus Crusade for Christ founder Dr. Bill Bright. I was part of Campus Crusade for Christ (now called Cru) when I was in college. In 1972, I attended Campus Crusade for Christ's Explo '72 at the Cotton Bowl in Dallas, Texas, and it was there that I dedicated my life to full-time Christian service.

In 1995, Dr. Bright issued his last global call. It was an unusual one from this strong evangelical leader. He challenged leaders around the globe to join him in a twenty-one-day fast with prayer for spiritual breakthrough. He released a prophetic proclamation and called for a time of consecration. His book *The Coming Revival* explores the predicament that

32. Tony Cauchi, "Franklin Hall," Revival Library, https://www.revival-library.org/revival_heroes/20th_century/hall_franklin.shtml.
33. Mahesh Chavda, *The Hidden Power of Prayer & Fasting* (Shippensburg, PA: Destiny Image Publishers, 1998).

the United States is in a moral freefall and the church is largely spiritually impotent. The solution? Seeking the Lord through fasting and prayer.[34] Dr. Bright stated, "Fasting is the most powerful spiritual discipline of all the Christian disciplines. Through fasting and prayer, the Holy Spirit can transform your life…. Fasting and prayer can bring about revival—a change in the direction of our nation, the nations of earth and the fulfillment of the Great Commission."[35]

Another such leader is one of my peers, Lou Engle, founder of The Call, now called The Send. In his book *The Jesus Fast*, Lou issued a passionate, prophetic summons to prayer and fasting. The book essentially talks about how we are poised at a key moment in history. There is pain and chaos in the world around us, but the tide of evil can be turned. Again, the solution lies in prayer and fasting, and our model in this endeavor is Jesus. Personal breakthroughs, historic revival, revelations of God's glory, and the ability to remove demonic hindrances are always preceded by God's people engaging in forty days of prayer and fasting. The world is filled with pride; in contrast, the church is called to fast in humility.[36]

I echo the preceding statement because this concept is definitely worth repeating: "The world is filled with pride; in contrast, the church is called to fast in humility."

In the first twenty or so years of my ministry, I did two twenty-one-day fasts every year; plus, I virtually fasted two days every week, and it was absolutely my delight. Then, as I mentioned previously, I went through some health issues, including hypoglycemia, so I couldn't do extensive fasting. Thankfully, though, over the past five years, I have been able to reengage in many different forms of fasting, such as the Daniel fast and intermittent fasting. Participating in such fasts brings so much happiness to my soul. You may think that's an unusual statement to make about fasting, but it really does bring my soul joy as I spend dedicated time with my heavenly Father. And from what we have just discussed about corporate

---

34. Bill Bright, *The Coming Revival: America's Call to Fast, Pray, and "Seek God's Face"* (Midlands, UK: New Life Publications, 1995). Dr. Bright was originally against speaking in tongues, but later in his ministry, he chose to lift the ban on the gifts of the Spirit. He also received a revelation vision about the importance of fasting.
35. Bright, *Coming Revival*.
36. Lou Engle and Dean Briggs, *The Jesus Fast: The Call to Awaken the Nations* (Ada, MI: Chosen Books, 2016).

fasting and prayer, we can expect not only personal joy through fasting but also forgiveness, healing, and widespread restoration.

THE "BRIDEGROOM FAST"

Ultimately, as Mike Bickle relates in his book *The Rewards of Fasting*, fasting brings us deeper into our relationship with our "Bridegroom God," who cherishes us so deeply that He is "lovesick" for us. This is what Mike and others refer to as the "Bridegroom Fast."

> *And Jesus said to them, "The attendants of the groom cannot mourn as long as the groom is with them, can they? But the days will come when the groom is taken away from them, and then they will fast."*
>
> (Matthew 9:15)

Mike expresses that Jesus knew His disciples had grown so accustomed to enjoying His presence that, after He was gone, they would mourn the loss of this fellowship and begin to yearn for a sense of closeness to Him. Yearning for the one you love is commonly called "lovesickness." Can you imagine wholehearted lovers of Jesus today becoming so filled with holy lovesickness that they freely choose to live a lifestyle of fasting? This is what Jesus was prophetically speaking about.

Here are three wonderful results of seeking our Bridegroom God with devotion and fasting:

1. You will receive more revelation of God while poring over His Word. Imagine receiving more revelation of the beauty of God that fascinates our hearts!

2. You will receive a greater measure of revelation in an accelerated way. When people tell me, "I just can't wait to receive more from God," I tell them to add fasting to their loving meditation on the Word. This type of fasting speeds up the process of receiving from God. It also accelerates the process of getting rid of old mindsets, old strongholds, and hard-heartedness.

3. The revelation we receive will touch us at a deeper level. A heart tenderized in love is the greatest gift the Holy Spirit can work in a worshipper. To live with a sense of being loved by God and feeling

a reciprocal, passionate love for Him is the most exhilarating form of existence. If you want to experience more of Jesus in a deeper way, start fasting with a focus on Jesus as the Bridegroom. The Holy Spirit gives grace and revelation to His people who aren't afraid to cry out for it. And when you respond to His wooing and embrace a Bridegroom fast—God's feast for His bride—you will mature and enter into intimacy with the Bridegroom. Then you will be able to assume your identity as the bride of Christ and be fully prepared for His return.[37]

THE OUTPOURING AND THE VISITATION

In this chapter, we have covered some significant aspects of fasting. In the book of Joel, we looked at the state of desolation, the prophetic promise of restoration, and the principles we can stand on to go from desolation to restoration—the principles of fasting and intercession. Individually, we are called to fast and pray by the Holy Spirit; corporately, we are called to pray by Spirit-filled local and national leaders. The cry is, "Save the people, O God, for Your honor." The purpose of fasting and prayer is to experience the outpouring of the Holy Spirit and the visitation of God in an unparalleled, historic manner. The end result is the fulfillment of Joel 2:28, 32:

> And afterward, **I will pour out my Spirit on all people**. Your sons and daughters will prophesy, your old men will dream dreams, your young men will see visions.… And **everyone who calls on the name of the LORD will be saved**; for on Mount Zion and in Jerusalem **there will be deliverance**, as the LORD has said, even among the survivors whom the LORD calls. (NIV)

LET'S PRAY TOGETHER

Our almighty God, if we're not desperate for restoration, make us desperate, whether it's for breakthrough in our personal lives or breakthrough in our communities. If we are complacent, change

---

37. See Mike Bickle and Dana Candler, *The Rewards of Fasting: Experiencing the Power and Affections of God* (Kansas City: MO: Forerunner Publishing, 2005), chapter 1, "The Bridegroom God," chapter 2, "Seven Types of Biblical Fasting," chapter 3, "Understanding the Bridegroom Fast," and chapter 5, "Fasting: Embracing Voluntary Weakness."

us. If we have fallen asleep on our watch, wake us up. Because sacrifice releases a greater dimension of Your power, lead us in the way that You would have us to fast and pray in this critical hour. We want to see revival breakthrough in our lives and in the lives of our families, as well as in our cities and in our nations. We volunteer freely to stand in the gap through prayer and fasting, knowing that these spiritual disciplines are keys to open big doors that release more of Your presence and power. Let us seek You, our Bridegroom God, with all our hearts. In Jesus's mighty name, Amen and Amen!

PART THREE:

THE POWER IN GOD'S PRESENCE

7

GATEKEEPERS OF HIS PRESENCE

"Better is one day in your courts than a thousand elsewhere;
I would rather be a doorkeeper in the house of my God than dwell
in the tents of the wicked. *For the* LORD *God is a sun and shield;*
the LORD *bestows favor and honor; no good thing does he withhold*
from those whose walk is blameless. LORD *Almighty,*
blessed is the one who trusts in you."
—Psalm 84:10–12 (NIV)

Now we begin the third part of this teaching on *Revival Breakthrough*, which concentrates on the power in God's presence. I love to discuss the subject of being gatekeepers of God's presence. I actually have only three goals in my life: (1) I want to teach people to pray. If I go to be with the Lord before the second coming of Jesus, I would like to go down in history as someone about whom people could say, "He was a man who prayed and taught others how to pray." (2) I would like to be known as a man who heard God and taught others how to hear God. (3) I would love for it to be true that I was a person who carried the presence of God and taught others how to be carriers of His great presence too.

With those goals at the forefront of my mind, I want to walk together with you through this chapter for God's glory. Our theme passage is Psalm 84:10–12, which includes the words *"Better is one day in your courts than a thousand elsewhere."* There's an old television commercial from the 1950s—one that doesn't apply to me at all today!—with the slogan, "A little dab'll do ya." It was an ad for Brylcreem, a hair-styling product that would slick back a guy's hair. Well, guess what? With God, a "little dab" of His presence does *not* do you. In fact, the more you receive, the more you want. And the more you receive, it doesn't "do you," it *undoes* you—but in a marvelous way! It releases you to enter into all that God is calling you to be and do. And that's what this chapter, "Gatekeepers of His Presence," is all about.

As always, let's begin with prayer:

Father, we are so grateful for what is written in Psalm 84. We desire that these verses might be exemplified in our lives. I ask that You would take the elements of this psalm and "plaster them" on us so that we can transfer this revelation to others—just as Jesus used mud on the blind man's eyes before he saw Your glory. Take the essence of this lesson and transform people's lives so they can rejoice in the power of Your presence. In Jesus's name, Amen and Amen.

THE IMPORTANCE OF GATES AND THE GREAT GATEKEEPER

When I moved from Kansas City to Nashville, for multiple reasons, for an entire year, I was fascinated with the subject of gates. So, I read about gates, and I studied gates. At the end of the year, I came up with an extremely simple conclusion about the function of gates that I have applied to the idea of being gatekeepers of God's presence. We'll be looking at opening and closing gates in realms of the Spirit and what that means with regard to revival breakthrough.

A gate can be defined as an entrance, a portal, a passageway, a doorway, a threshold, or an opening. Natural gates serve two primary purposes: (1) When they are closed, their function is to keep people or things out. (2) When they are open, their function is to allow people or things to enter. As it is in the natural, so it is in the spiritual. Closed spiritual gates keep out the enemy and his schemes. Open spiritual gates bring heaven to earth.

In the Word of God, there are many references to gates and gatekeepers—or, to use the word in our opening Scripture passage, "doorkeepers."

But there is a Gatekeeper mentioned in Genesis who is the Greatest of all, and it is through Him that we can be gatekeepers of the Father's presence. Let's unfold how we are meant to follow the pattern of this mighty Gatekeeper.

When God told Abraham He was going to bless him, He mentioned a significant type of "gate":

> Indeed I will greatly bless you, and I will greatly multiply your seed as the stars of the heavens and as the sand, which is on the seashore; and **your seed shall possess the gate of their enemies**. And in your seed all the nations of the earth shall be blessed, because you have obeyed My voice. (Genesis 22:17–18)

In conjunction with this passage, note that Galatians 3:16 states, "*Now the promises were spoken to Abraham and **to his seed**. He does not say, 'And to seeds,' as one would in referring to many, but rather as in referring to one, 'And to your seed,' **that is, Christ**.*" Jesus Christ was the Seed mentioned in Genesis 22. The "*seed*" was referenced in the Old Testament, but the fulfillment was revealed in the New Testament.

What is the significance that the promises were spoken to Abraham and to his "*seed*," singular? Jesus, the Seed, possesses the gate of the enemy, having overcome death, hell, and Satan by His crucifixion and resurrection. What this meant is that the power of the blessing promised to Abraham and fulfilled through Christ would flow to such an extent that it would completely overtake the curse that was upon humankind as a result of the fall.

Now, remember that phrase "*possess the gate of their enemies*" from Genesis 22? It becomes important because we, too, are to possess what Christ has redeemed for us—even the gate of the enemy. Again, a gate is an entrance, a portal, a passageway, a doorway, a threshold, or an opening, and we are to take back and possess the gate the enemy has stolen. With the battering ram of Jesus's victorious name, we are to open spiritual gates that historically have been closed. Jesus said, "*And I also say to you that you are Peter, and upon this rock **I will build My church; and the gates of Hades will not overpower it**"* (Matthew 16:18), and "*Behold, I have given you authority…over all the power of the enemy*" (Luke 10:19).

Jesus is the Victor who has already overcome. According to Revelation 1:18, He has taken from the enemy *"the keys of death and of Hades."* He has already accomplished this, and He has given us the keys the enemy stole. Remember that gates are used either to keep people and things out or to allow people and things in. Consider this: small keys open big doors or gates. Let's learn to how to insert spiritual keys to unlock gates for God's glory to be manifested and for captives to be set free, as well as to use keys to lock evil gates shut, preventing the enemy from entering and bringing destruction.

OPEN GATES TO HEAVEN[38]

Sometimes, our sole focus is on the dark gates of the demonic world, but we must remember that there are good gates—portals, doorways to the heavenly world, to God's kingdom—that He wants us to access. These gates can be attitudes and actions that open heaven to us, including thanksgiving, sacrifice, and praise. Psalm 100:4 says, *"**Enter His gates** with thanksgiving, and His courtyards with praise. Give thanks to Him, bless His name."* We enter into the kingdom of God, and into our Lord's presence, as we experience *"righteousness and peace and joy in the Holy Spirit"* (Romans 14:17).

Here are some biblical references to people who experiencing open gates to the heavenlies:

Ezekiel 1:1–4 unwraps a fascinating dimension of what Ezekiel saw when the heavens were opened to him: *"**The heavens were opened** and I saw visions of God.... As I looked, behold, a high wind was coming from the north, a great cloud with fire flashing intermittently and a bright light around it, and in its midst something like gleaming metal in the midst of the fire."*

Acts 7:55–56 reveals Stephen's experience with God's presence while being stoned to death for Christ's sake: *"But he, being full of the Holy Spirit, looked intently into heaven and saw the glory of God, and Jesus standing at the right hand of God; and he said, '**Behold, I see the heavens opened** and the Son of Man standing at the right hand of God.'"*

---

38. I teach much more about heavenly gates in my book *The Seer* and its related online classes, where I talk about the key of intimacy to open heaven, as well as other intriguing aspects of this topic. Visit https://godencounters.com/classes/the-seer/.

Revelation 4:1–2 describes what John the Beloved, while imprisoned on the Isle of Patmos, saw at the threshold of heaven: *"After these things I looked, and behold, **a door standing open in heaven**, and the first voice which I had heard, like the sound of a trumpet speaking with me, said, 'Come up here, and I will show you what must take place after these things.' Immediately I was in the Spirit; and behold, a throne was standing in heaven, and someone was sitting on the throne."*

John was alone in exile, but he was not really alone, because he was taken into God's presence. (I have experienced the same reality of being alone but not alone. That is why I chose for my debut music album the title *Never Alone*. I hope you have experienced God's presence in the same way.)

When John wrote the book of Revelation, he was about eighty years old. He was meditating on the things of God on the Lord's Day when he heard a *"voice,"* and a door to heaven opened. John was shown *"someone… sitting on the throne."* He went into great detail about the Someone, the throne, the elders, and more. I encourage you to read the entire fourth chapter of Revelation and meditate on those spiritual realities.[39]

Genesis 28:10–17, describing the open portal Jacob experienced, is one of my favorite passages:

> *Then Jacob departed from Beersheba and went toward Haran. And he happened upon a particular place and spent the night there, because the sun had set; and he took one of the stones of the place and made it a support for his head, and lay down in that place. And he had a dream, and behold, a ladder was set up on the earth with its top reaching to heaven; and behold, the angels of God were ascending and descending on it. Then behold, the LORD was standing above it and said, "I am the LORD, the God of your father Abraham and the God of Isaac; the land on which you lie I will give to you and to your descendants. Your descendants will also be like the dust of the earth, and you will spread out to the west and to the east, and to the north and to the south; and in you and in your descendants shall all the families of the earth be blessed. Behold, I am with you and will keep you wherever you go, and will bring you back to this land; for I will not leave you until I have*

---

39. You can read more about this incredible look into heaven in my books *Praying with God's Heart* (Ada, MI: Chosen Books, 2018) and *The Seer*.

done what I have promised you." Then Jacob awoke from his sleep and said, "The LORD *is certainly in this place, and I did not know it!" And he was afraid and said, "How awesome is this place!* **This is none other than the house of God, and this is the gate of heaven!"**

In this passage, the Holy Spirit lighted upon Jacob after the patriarch had paused from his journey for the night. Jacob lay down in the desert with a rock as his pillow. I have often asked people struggling with their spiritual walk, "Have you ever lived between a rock and a hard place?" That is where Jacob was—at a dry, rocky, hard place. However, that setting became a place of visitation for him, a place where God met him. As he lay in that place in the desert, a heavenly ladder came down, and *"the* LORD *was standing above it."*

It's fascinating that the Bible says, *"Angels of God were ascending and descending on"* the ladder. Because they ascended *and* descended, perhaps they were involved in helping to carry prayers to the One at the top of the ladder. Obviously, angels aren't only in heaven, but they are on earth as well. The Lord's angelic host is already here! And His messengers come from heaven to earth through open spiritual portals.

Jacob woke up after having had this amazing dream, and he said, in essence, "Surely God is in this place, and I didn't have a clue!" I believe that point is one of God's revelations to us in this Scripture passage. He wants us to realize that He is with us in the place of our assignment. God desires to give us spiritual life; He wants to give us redemptive interpretation and understanding for the place in which we currently dwell.

We may feel like we're between a rock and a hard place, but God is ready and willing to bring us revelation even in that difficult circumstance so that we can say, as Jacob did, *"How awesome is this place! This is none other than the house of God, and this is the gate of heaven!"*

This account signifies that before we experience revival breakthrough in the natural, we have to see it and obtain it in the spiritual. We have to call on the Lord, *"who gives life to the dead and calls those things which do not exist as though they did"* (Romans 4:17 NKJV). We need the eyes of the Lord to have a proper spiritual understanding of the place where we dwell and to see the gates of heaven. When we do, everything around us changes. With our spiritual eyes, we see through God's redemptive lens. We see His purpose, His plans, and His destiny.

ENTERING THE GATES

In what ways can we enter such heavenly gates into God's presence and receive His revelation? Scripture expresses a number of ways. We can enter through...

+ **Praise:** *"But you will call your walls salvation, and your gates praise"* (Isaiah 60:18).

+ **Worship:** *"Therefore, since we receive a kingdom which cannot be shaken, let's show gratitude, by which we may offer to God an acceptable service with reverence and awe"* (Hebrews 12:28).

+ **Sacrifice:** *"The sacrifices of God are a broken spirit; a broken and a contrite heart, God, You will not despise"* (Psalm 51:17).

+ **Thanksgiving:** *"Enter His gates with thanksgiving, and His courtyards with praise. Give thanks to Him, bless His name"* (Psalm 100:4).

+ **Unity:** *"How good and pleasant it is when God's people live together in unity! It is like precious oil poured on the head, running down on the beard, running down on Aaron's beard, down on the collar of his robe. It is as if the dew of Hermon were falling on Mount Zion. For there the LORD bestows his blessing, even life forevermore"* (Psalm 133:1–3 NIV).

+ **Giving:** *"At Caesarea there was a man named Cornelius, a centurion in what was known as the Italian Regiment. He and all his family were devout and God-fearing; he gave generously to those in need and prayed to God regularly. One day at about three in the afternoon he had a vision. He distinctly saw an angel of God, who came to him and said, 'Cornelius!' Cornelius stared at him in fear. 'What is it, Lord?' he asked. The angel answered, 'Your prayers and gifts to the poor have come up as a memorial offering before God'"* (Acts 10:1–4 NIV).

+ **Death:** *"For to me, to live is Christ and to die is gain. If I am to go on living in the body, this will mean fruitful labor for me. Yet what shall I choose? I do not know! I am torn between the two: I desire to depart and be with Christ, which is better by far; but it is more necessary for* you that I remain in the body. Convinced of this, I know that I will remain, and I will continue with all of you for your progress and joy in the faith" (Philippians 1:21–25 NIV).

BREAKERS WHO OPEN THE WAY

As we develop a lifestyle of coming into God's presence, we can receive His anointing as a "breaker" for His kingdom. Micah 2:13 says,

> **The One who breaks open the way** will go up before them; **they will break through the gate and go out.** Their King will pass through before them, the **LORD at their head.** (NIV)

Years ago, I was praying in the gift of tongues for many hours a day, a pattern that lasted for weeks, in order to hear from God about the forerunners who would go before to open the way for revival in New York City. At the time, I was unaware of this verse in Micah, and I sent a letter to Dick Simmons, asking if he could help me understand who would be these forerunners to pave the way.

When Dick received my letter, he was actually praying from Micah 2:13, and he was asking himself, "Where are the breakers who will go before, who will break open the way...for New York City?" So, when he read my letter, he called me on the phone and said, "How would you like to go to New York City?" I had never been to the Big Apple. I didn't have any money to go. I didn't even have a salary at that time, but I did have a wife and two children to support. Yet I said to him, "Sure. Why not?" The Lord provided, and that trip set the course of my life on an entirely new journey. This section reveals the principles I learned concerning Micah 2:13.

At that time, Tommy Tenney's profound book *God Chasers* had not even been published yet, but the Holy Spirit spoke to Tommy to attend a Catch the Fire conference in Cleveland, Ohio. I had been asked to be the opening speaker at this conference, and I felt an urging from the Lord to accept the invitation. Being the first speaker at a conference is not exactly my forte; I prefer to come later, but sometimes I am called to be the forerunner, or the breaker.

Before the conference started, I was in my hotel room going over what I had planned to present. But then I had an "aha!" moment in the Spirit.

Within five minutes, I had changed my topic to Micah 2:13. I left my room, went to the session at the conference venue, and started teaching. There was a man sitting in the front row whom I didn't know, but my eyes kept glancing toward him. I found out later that it was Tommy Tenney and that Micah 2:13 was the specific verse on which he was establishing his entire life ministry about the bread of God's presence and the breaker anointing.

We ended up spending hours together sharing the Word and our faith. Subsequently, Tommy was used in Baltimore, Maryland, to hold three straight years of sustained meetings. I was invited to participate because we were preaching an identical message, although we had never met or compared notes before that day at the conference.

Here are many of the principles I have learned about the breaker anointing:

1. There is no breakthrough without a breaker. Jesus is our Breaker.

2. We are to flow in the path of our prophetic pioneer, Jesus.

3. Breakers pass through the gates and break open the way.

4. God is looking for pioneer "point people" to break open the way like bulldozers in the Holy Spirit.

5. Breakers are like those who travail for the purpose of opening or broadening the opening of the birth canal so that birth can occur.

6. Breakers are used and anointed to open the way by breaking open the gates of the enemy and taking possession of what Satan has stolen. They create more room and more space in the spiritual realm for the King and His kingdom to manifest.

7. A relevant breaker Scripture is Isaiah 58:12: "*Your people will rebuild the ancient ruins and will raise up the age-old foundations; you will be called Repairer of Broken Walls, Restorer of Streets with Dwellings*" (NIV). Breakers often open the way to renewal and restoration.

8. Isaiah 62:10–12 complements the above verse by adding, "*Pass through, **pass through the gates!** Prepare the way for the people. Build up, build up the highway! Remove the stones. Raise a banner for the nations. The LORD has made proclamation to the ends of the earth:*

'Say to Daughter Zion, "See, your Savior comes! See, his reward is with him, and his recompense accompanies him."' They will be called the Holy People, the Redeemed of the LORD; and you will be called Sought After, the City No Longer Deserted" (NIV).

Psalm 24 expresses the first messianic prophecy in the Bible concerning the historic moment when the King of Glory, Jesus Christ, would possess the "keys" and be welcomed into heaven:

Lift up your heads, you gates; be lifted up, you ancient doors, that the King of glory may come in. *Who is this King of glory? The* LORD *strong and mighty, the* LORD *mighty in battle.* **Lift up your heads, you gates; lift them up, you ancient doors, that the King of glory may come in.** (Psalm 24:7–9 NIV)

According to accurate biblical teachings and Hebraic understandings and commentaries, this passage depicts the antiphonal exchange of two choirs of angels. One choir is singing, *"Lift up your heads, you gates."* And the other one responds, *"Lift up your heads, you gates; be lifted up, you ancient doors, that the King of glory may come in."* Then the first choir sings, *"Who is this King of glory?"* And the other choir sings, *"The* LORD *strong and mighty, the* LORD *mighty in battle."* Again, this is called antiphonal intercession or antiphonal worship. It is quite beautiful.

Similarly, we are to be in antiphonal agreement with the *"great cloud of witnesses"* (Hebrews 12:1) that heaven would be manifested on earth. To do this, we must know in our hearts that God is the King of Glory, the Lord, strong and mighty! In like manner, our prayers become, "Open the way for the great visitation. Let the gateways be open from heaven to earth for the power and the glory of His presence. And may God's angelic army be released to come to earth to assist us in fulfilling our assignments." Praying such prayers are part of the role of a breaker.

Proverbs 31:23 tells us, *"Her husband is respected at the city gate, where he takes his seat among the elders of the land"* (NIV). It is my conviction that, in these times, as the Spirit moves in our midst, church and city governments will take on new understandings about being gatekeepers of God's presence. Church leaders and Christian marketplace leaders will seek God to know who and what to let in and who and what to forbid entrance into the life of the church or the city. Enemies of God will be recognized, and gatekeepers will work together to build the kingdom.

John 10:7–9 says, "*Therefore Jesus said again, 'Very truly I tell you, I am the gate for the sheep. All who have come before me are thieves and robbers, but the sheep have not listened to them. I am the gate; whoever enters through me will be saved. They will come in and go out, and find pasture'*" (NIV). Jesus will be honored as the Chief Gatekeeper in our midst, and all other gatekeepers will honor His leadership and submit to Him.

SHARING THE KEYS

Knowledge about spiritual keys and open gates is not just information to be gathered for our own curiosity but rather truth to be shared with others. Jesus warned,

> *Woe to you experts in the law, because you have taken away the key to knowledge. You yourselves have not entered, and you have hindered those who were entering.* (Luke 11:52 NIV)

God gives us keys of revelation or knowledge to use for His glory and our benefit so that we can help expand and advance His kingdom. Unfortunately, some people who have been given stewardship of keys keep them only for themselves. They call them "secrets" and hide them away, forbidding or preventing others from using them. But if you have been given a revelation, then that revelation is not just for you. *Revelations are to give away so many people can reap the spiritual rewards God intended.* You must use the keys to enter into the gates of heaven yourself, breaking open the way so that many others can pass over into that place as well.

The key to knowledge you've received must be accompanied by brokenness. When spiritual humility or brokenness and revelation are brought together, authority is released. Where there is authority, there is impartation and change. This is what it means to walk in the lifestyle of the Sermon on the Mount that Jesus taught! Live like Jesus; you'll have authority like Jesus!

Look for ways in which God can use you to open the gates to His presence for others. One time, when I was in the Czech Republic right after communism was lifted, I was ministering to hundreds of new believers in

Christ Jesus. I don't remember exactly what I was talking about, but while the interpreter was translating whatever I had said, the Holy Spirit said to me, "Have you ever considered the multidirectional dimension of prayer?" I thought, "What?" I didn't understand what He meant, so I just continued with my teaching.

However, this happened several times. The Holy Spirit kept asking me, "Have you ever considered the multidirectional dimension of prayer?" Well, of course, I hadn't. Again, I didn't even know what He was talking about, and He kept interrupting me! I was thinking, "Hey, You know that I'm on assignment right now. I have to think fast and respond fast because I'm in front of a couple thousand people." Guess what? The Holy Spirit didn't mind. After all, He's in charge, and He doesn't really care if I finish what I think I'm supposed to finish or not.

This was just like the night when I was the opening speaker at the Catch the Fire Conference in Cleveland, Ohio, when He gave me a download in five minutes, and I changed my subject to the breaker anointing. The Holy Spirit then said to me, "Tell My people that what goes up comes back down." I immediately thought, "Oh my goodness, thank You! You just gave me the most brilliant theology on prayer that I have ever heard. I had never thought of it in that way. 'What goes up comes back down.' Oh! The angels ascend *and* they descend, bringing God's answers to people's prayers." I gave the people at the conference this word. It was a message that would enable God's people to better enter into His presence through prayer, with a greater expectation that He would hear and answer.

Another time, I was in London, England, ministering at the London Prayer Summit. I was trying to present material on "The Gatekeepers of His Presence," but I kept looking over to the side where a particular man was sitting. Every time I did, I heard phrases going through my mind that sounded like "Yabba-dabba-doo." It was so distracting that I purposely positioned my body to look in the opposite direction so I could concentrate. Yet my body was magnetically being drawn to look at this man, and then these phrases would rumble around inside my head. It made no sense to me.

I became so annoyed by what was happening that I got off the stage, went over to the man, and said to him in what I thought was gibberish:

"Your name is Conrad, and you are from Allahabad in India, near the Ganges River. You just spent all the money you had to come here to this conference so you could pick up the presence of God and take it back to the place where people go to dip themselves in the Ganges River to get cleansed from their sins. You want to establish a House of Prayer filled with His presence there."

Finally, those "Yabba-dabba-doo" words were out of my head. I prayed for the man, and he was resting in the Spirit for the next several hours.

The next morning, when I was having breakfast at the hotel, the lobby elevator opened, and the man from the meeting walked out, came up to me, and said, "How did you know my name?"

I replied, "I don't."

He said, "Yes, you do."

I said, "No, I don't."

He insisted, "Yes, you do. Yesterday you called me by name, and you told me what city I'm from, Allahabad on the Ganges River in India. My name is Conrad, and you even pronounced it with a proper British-Indian Accent!"

It was amazing! He went home with what he came for—the presence of God and encouragement to start a House of Prayer on the Ganges River!

I am here to tell you that *you* can be the next Gatekeeper of His presence. Just remain open to the Holy Spirit's leading, and see what He will do!

THE BRILLIANCE OF HIS GREAT PRESENCE

As we enter into God's gates—through praise, worship, sacrifice, thanksgiving, unity, giving, and death—the brilliance of His great presence will shine before us. For an illustration of this, let's return to the conversation between Moses and the Lord from Exodus 33, which we looked at briefly in chapter 1:

> *"If you are pleased with me,* **teach me your ways** *so I may know you and continue to find favor with you. Remember that this nation is your people."* The LORD replied, **"My Presence will go with you, and I will**

give you rest." Then Moses said to him, "If your Presence does not go with us, do not send us up from here. How will anyone know that you are pleased with me and with your people unless you go with us? What else will distinguish me and your people from all the other people on the face of the earth?" And the LORD said to Moses, "I will do the very thing you have asked, because I am pleased with you and I know you by name." Then Moses said, "Now show me your glory." And the LORD said, "I will cause all my goodness to pass in front of you, and I will proclaim my name, the LORD, in your presence. I will have mercy on whom I will have mercy, and I will have compassion on whom I will have compassion. But," he said, "you cannot see my face, for no one may see me and live." Then the LORD said, "There is a place near me where you may stand on a rock. When my glory passes by, I will put you in a cleft in the rock and cover you with my hand until I have passed by. Then I will remove my hand and you will see my back; but my face must not be seen."   (Exodus 33:13–23 NIV)

There are so many spiritual applications to having God's great presence in our midst. I had an experience that brought this truth home to me. One time, when I was "resting" in the Lord's presence, the Holy Spirit said, "I want to teach you to release the highest weapon of spiritual warfare." I continued to listen because I knew there must be more, and I was eager to hear what He had to say on this subject that I had studied for years. He continued, "I will teach you to release the brilliance of My presence."

In a moment, it seemed like all my theological questions about spiritual warfare had been answered. What is the highest weapon of spiritual warfare? God is! He wants us to be gatekeepers so we can release the brilliance of His great presence throughout our sphere of influence and beyond!

The call for gatekeepers of His presence is going forth. I shared some unusual but true stories in this chapter, and you can have amazing experiences and then share about them as well. I am not here to exalt Tommy Tenney or Mahesh Chavda or James Goll. I'm here to exalt the one Man, Christ Jesus, and I offer you the invitation He offered me: "I want to teach you how to release the highest weapon of spiritual warfare, the brilliance of My presence."

ONLY HE CAN SATISFY

As I expressed at the beginning of this book, in our day, the Holy Spirit is looking for modern-day Simeons and Annas who will minister in God's temple and be forerunners, those who welcome the manifest presence of Jesus. "If they wait, He will come" is a phrase that we must not only hear but act upon.

Once you have truly tasted the goodness of the Lord's presence, nothing else will satisfy you. You are ruined for the rest of your life—for Him. *It's true.* Oh, how I have found it to be true! Pour out your heart to Him and seek His presence. One day within His courts is better than the best this world could ever offer. Tell the Lord now that you want to be a gatekeeper of His presence.

LET'S PRAY TOGETHER

Heavenly Father, we come into Your gates with thanksgiving and into Your courts with the sacrifice of praise. We love You, and we find our delight in You. We declare that the chief goal and aim of our lives is to be doorkeepers in Your house. Like Moses, we want to carry the distinguishing characteristic of the people of God— Your very presence. Hear the cry of our hearts, O Lord and Savior. We set ourselves apart to be gatekeepers of Your most brilliant presence. We pray this in Jesus's mighty name. Amen and Amen.

8

POSSESSED BY GOD

"But you are a chosen people, a royal priesthood, a holy nation,
a people for God's own possession, so that you may proclaim the
excellencies of Him who has called you out of darkness
into His marvelous light."
—1 Peter 2:9

Some people might consider this particular chapter to be the most contro-versial—or the most contagious—of the entire book. Our theme verse is 1 Peter 2:9, which includes the phrase *"But you are a chosen people."* Certain Bible versions, like the *English Standard Version*, use the word *"race"* rather than *"people."* This verse begins with the phrase *"But you are..."*—express-ing all that we are as God's beloved children through Jesus Christ. To allow these truths to move into our minds and hearts, let's read this verse again, putting that initial phrase in front of each one of the specific descriptions included in it:

But you are a chosen people ["race"].

But you are...a royal priesthood.

But you are…a holy nation.

But you are…a people for God's own possession, so that you may proclaim the excellencies of Him who has called you out of darkness into His marvelous light.

Revival breakthrough will occur as we fully enter into our relationship with God as His chosen people, His royal priesthood, His holy nation, and a people for His own possession. Let me now pray for you that, as you read this chapter, you will come to more fully understand these spiritual realities and allow the Lord to manifest them in your life to His glory.

Father, thank You for such a time as this. Lord, I present myself to You, and I present all those who are reading this book to You. I ask that Your invisible hand would reach into hearts and souls and do what only You can do: impart Your wisdom and grace to each one. I ask that You, Holy Spirit, whom Jesus called *"the finger of God"* [Luke 11:20], would now come and touch each of us in a personal way. We believe that You are capable and willing and that You will do exceedingly, abundantly above all that we ask in faith. In Jesus's name, Amen and Amen.

WHAT DOES IT MEAN TO BE "GOD'S OWN POSSESSION"?

Rodney Howard-Browne was a missionary from South Africa to the United States. I met with him on a few occasions, one of which I will describe shortly. Pastor Rodney has been quoted as saying, "Those whom God is using today is not because they are anyone's vessel but because they have touched God and God has touched them." I can relate to that theology—and I can relate to our God who is like that.

To unfold what it means to be the Father's own possession, filled with His life, we will begin by looking at the example of an individual from church history who had firsthand experience with such intimacy with God: Charles G. Finney, whom I quoted in an earlier chapter on fasting. Finney (1792–1875) was instrumental in the Second Great Awakening, an American revival in the mid-1800s. He was a lawyer before he became a fabled evangelist, and he was referred to as a "logician on fire." I find that designation quite fascinating, indicating the blending of his natural gifts with the fire of the Holy Spirit to win souls for Christ.

The following is a quote by Finney that reveals his earnest and passionate love for the Lord:

> There was no fire and no light in the room; hence, it was dark. Nevertheless, it appeared to me as if it was perfectly light.
>
> As I went in and shut the door after me, it seemed as if I met the Lord Jesus Christ face to face. It did not occur to me then, nor did it for some time afterward, that it was wholly a mental state. On the contrary, it seemed to me that I met Him face to face and saw Him as I would see any other man. He said nothing, but looked at me in such a manner as to break me right down at His feet. I have always since regarded this as a most remarkable state of mind, for it seemed to me a reality that He stood before me and that I fell down at His feet and poured out my soul to Him. I wept aloud like a child, and made such confessions as I could with my choked utterance. It seemed to me as if I bathed His feet with my tears....[40]

This experience continued for a lengthy period of time. Finney describes what happened next:

> ...The Holy Spirit descended upon me in a manner that seemed to go through me, body and soul. I could feel the impression, like a wave of electricity, going through and through me. Indeed it seemed to come in waves, and waves of liquid love—for I could not express it in any other way. And yet it did not seem like water, but rather as the breath of God. I can recollect distinctly that it seemed to fan me like immense wings; and it seemed to me, as these waves passed over me, that they literally moved my hair like a passing breeze.
>
> No words can express the wonderful love that was shed abroad in my heart. It seemed to me that I should burst. I wept aloud with

---

40. Charles Finney, *The Memoirs of Charles G. Finney*, 1868, https://www.charlesgfinney.com/memoirsrestored/memrest02.htm.

joy and love, and I do not know but I should say I literally bellowed out the unutterable gushings of my heart. These waves came over me, and over me, and over me one after the other, until I recollect I cried out, "I shall die if these waves continue to pass over me." I said to the Lord, "Lord, I cannot bear any more." Yet I had no fear of death....

In this state I was taught the doctrine of justification by faith as a present experience.... I could now see and understand what was meant by the passage, "Being justified by faith, we have peace with God through our Lord Jesus Christ."[41]

I believe that Charles Finney was "possessed by God." His experience gives us a window into what God is calling us to in our relationship with Him: first, full surrender; then, possession by Love Himself.

I want to relate a corresponding experience that I had. Once, while I was at a conference in Charlotte, North Carolina, I experienced an interactive vision in which I was invited to come up higher into God's presence by ascending a staircase leading up into heaven. As I climbed the stairs, the higher I ascended, the more I was enveloped in a beautiful white-light mist of His brilliant, great presence shining all around. Eventually, I came to a plateau where there was only piercing white light penetrating my whole being—in me, through me, above me, and all around me. I began to sob and to cry out as the light of God and His revelation saturated me. All I could say was, "You're beautiful, You're beautiful, You're beautiful!"

I was experiencing another level of God's majesty and beauty, and I was filled with awe and wonder for who He is. Light pierced through my being, and if there was any hint of darkness, it had to flee. I thought, "How could anyone hold anything back from this God of amazing love?" He knew all my faults and yet totally loved me! I was consumed with the revelation of His transcendent majesty. I was radically overwhelmed and taken over by the beauty of who He is. I sobbed and sobbed and kept proclaiming, "You're beautiful!"

To be possessed by God is to be completely taken by His glory, holiness, and love. This is a key element of revival breakthrough.

---

41. Finney, *Memoirs.*

CAUGHT UP IN GOD'S MAJESTY AND BEAUTY

I next want to share another personal encounter I had with the Lord and with His precious servants who have helped me to comprehend the link between being possessed by God and bringing heaven to earth in revival.

Evan Roberts, whom we talked about in an earlier chapter about prayer, was a Welsh intercessor and revivalist. In 1998, I was privileged to be a part of a team that ministered on site at Moriah Chapel in southern Wales where the historic revival under young Roberts' leadership took place in 1904.

The day of our meetings, a carpenter was working in his attic, expanding it to create a new room in his house, and a secular newspaper from 1904 fell out of the wall. Its headline was "Roberts' Soul in Travail." It told about how the Holy Spirit took control of Roberts and seized him with the burden for lost souls. Roberts actually passed out in front of everyone, and they thought he might have died. Instead, out of travail, he had fallen into a trance, which he later came out of. This was when Evan Roberts received heaven's mandate for a hundred thousand souls to come to faith. Evan Roberts' key to revival breakthrough? He was overwhelmed or possessed by God with the spirit of prayer for lost souls. Do it again, Lord!

The carpenter brought this newspaper to our meeting that evening and showed it to us. When I looked at the article, it gripped my soul. And, during the meeting that same evening, I was taken up in the Spirit and given a promise. The Lord told me, "You are laboring for a worldwide release of the Holy Spirit." I came back from the vision and saw what was going on in the meeting, and then I was taken up in the Spirit again. This happened three times. The last time, the Holy Spirit said, "You're a friend of God, and you are laboring before Me for a worldwide embrace of the Holy Spirit." Whoa, that was fascinating. And it happened by my getting pricked by Evan Roberts' testimony about when his soul was in travail. While God is doing a new thing in revival today, we can still be powerfully influenced, through the Spirit, by those in the past who allowed themselves to be possessed by God for His purposes in awakening and abundant harvest.

GIDEON'S REWARD: CLOTHED AND POSSESSED BY GOD

Another vivid picture of being possessed by God, filled with the power of His Spirit, comes in the account of Gideon in the Old Testament. In the fall of 1993, the Lord permitted me to have three months where I spent several hours a day praying and worshipping in the gift of tongues. After this, I ministered at an intercessory prayer conference in Vancouver, British Columbia, Canada, on the topic of "Fire on the Altar," which I had never taught before. While I was there, a prophetic friend and I fell into travail on the floor at the same time. I was deep in intercession, and the Holy Spirit said to me, "Read Judges 6:34 from the *Amplified Bible*."

I don't read the *Amplified Bible*, so I said, "Read it from the *Amplified Bible?* I don't even have one." But then I noticed my wife's *Amplified Bible Classic Edition* under the seat next to mine. I picked it up, quickly turned to Judges 6:34, and read, *"But the Spirit of the Lord clothed Gideon with Himself and **took possession** of him…."*

That experience was another major confirmation for me about God's desire to completely fill our lives. This is God's way: possessing His people by His Spirit. Being possessed by God was Gideon's reward for tearing down the idolatrous high places that his father had set up. Gideon knew he would face retribution from his father's household and the men of the city if he did that, so he had to overcome his fear of persecution and danger. Despite that threat, he tore down the altars, and God responded by *"cloth*[ing] *Gideon with Himself."* I love that!

No wonder Gideon had authority to call forth thousands of fighting men and then bring them to the river to reduce their number to three hundred who had no common ground with fear. (See Judges 6:11–7:22.) It was because Gideon had had the fear driven out of his own life. You want a biblical basis for the idea of being possessed by God? Here it is: *"But the Spirit of the Lord clothed Gideon with Himself and took possession of him."* And this happened even before Jesus's death, resurrection, ascension, and sending of the Spirit on Pentecost.

INVADED BY HIS PRESENCE

Always remember that life is about God; it's not about us. He is greater than our weaknesses, and He is greater than all our excuses. God wants to consume us with His love and power, but it is not our ability or goodness that will make this happen. It is our full surrender to Him. Joel 3:10 says, *"Let the weakling say, 'I am strong!'"* (NIV). You are more than a conqueror through God's strength. Remember that. God will always provide for you, no matter what He calls you to do. Here are a few examples of this truth from the Bible:

- When God called Moses to lead His people out of Egypt, Moses protested, in effect, "But I stutter," so God gave him Aaron to be his mouthpiece. (See Exodus 4:1–17.)

- When Isaiah the prophet cried out, *"I am a man of unclean lips, and I live among a people of unclean lips,"* God sent an angel with fire to purge him. (See Isaiah 6:1–7.)

- When Jeremiah said, "But I am but a youth," the Lord revealed His sovereignty, told Jeremiah, "I knew you before you were ever born," and put His words in Jeremiah's mouth. (See Jeremiah 1:1–10.)

I have seen firsthand God's remarkable provision in this way, most memorably within my own family. Bob Jones, a seer prophet, came to me one day and said, "I saw your wife today in a vision, and she'll be the first of three hundred women who will be released into the prophetic." I really didn't understand what dear Bob Jones was saying, even though I was the doorkeeper to my house. So, like Mary in the Bible, I pondered in my heart what he had said. (See Luke 2:19.)

Then, in 1992, on the Day of Atonement, at one minute before midnight, when Michal Ann and I were both asleep, a lightning bolt crashed in our backyard. The light from it streaked through our closed bedroom window, and a man came and stood at the end of our bed. I immediately woke up and saw the man and a ball of fire (light supernaturally illuminated our bedroom for the next five hours). That man looked at me and said, "Watch your wife. I'm about to speak to her."

At that point, the manifested appearance of the angelic messenger dissipated, but the manifested Presence increased. Michal Ann woke up trembling and shaking in the presence of God. I whispered to her, "Ann, an angel has just come."

This was not our first angelic visitation. For whatever reason, every time we experienced this kind of exchange, I would whisper the news to my wife, in the fear of the Lord, so that she knew. I did not tell her what the angel had said. For the next twenty-four minutes, we trembled in bed together. We prayed for confirmation and for the Lord to show us what He wanted us to do. His presence drew near for nine straight weeks from midnight to 5:00 a.m., and it did not center on me but on Michal Ann.

One night, angels showed up, put their hands upon her back, and shoved the fear of man and the fear of rejection out of her. This transformed her from being a "Betty Crocker homemaker" into a "lioness" for God. It changed our relationship; it changed a little bit of everything in our lives. However, Michal Ann learned to ask for more of God, and she was determined. Whether she lived or died was not the issue. She continued to cry out to the Lord to draw near. One night, twenty-nine fireballs circulated in the bedroom, and they would come down and hit her, yet she would say, "Lord, send more." And He would come to her gently in the night season and sing over her.

I'm here to tell you that I observed how God consumed Michal Ann with His presence and changed her. I can testify to how God took control and made her into a fiery one.[42] When God takes possession of you, He will transform you into a vessel for His purposes too.

TANGIBLE ANOINTING

Earlier, I mentioned evangelist Rodney Howard-Browne. In another season of the movements of the Holy Spirit, I attended a meeting in St. Louis in which Pastor Rodney was speaking. There, I witnessed the raw, tangible anointing that rested upon his life and ministry. I was desperately hungry for more of God, so, in the middle of the meeting, as Pastor

---

42. For more on this life-transforming time, see James and Michal Ann Goll, *Heroines of Faith: Women of Courage, Compassion, and the Secret Place*, Women on the Frontlines series (Franklin, TN: God Encounters Ministries, 2021). This book combines three books previously released as *A Call to Courage*, *A Call to Compassion*, and *A Call to the Secret Place*.

Rodney was laying hands on the leaders at the front, I started lifting a loud cry for the Lord to visit me.

I cried out repeatedly, "Over here, right now!" I continued to cry out to the Lord until the man of God made his way toward me and eventually laid his hand upon me. I fell into a trance, and the voice of the Lord came to me, saying, "I commission you to write transferrable concepts, books, study manuals. I want you to ground My people in My Word and Spirit." Out of desperation to receive more of the anointing of the Holy Spirit, I received an impartation and commission for something I did not even know I was called to: writing and publishing. Again, as you seek the Lord's presence, you will discover more about what God has commissioned you to do.

A LIFE-CHANGING MOMENT WITH SAMUEL HOWELLS

I am especially excited to share this final testimony about what it means to be possessed by God. Many dedicated intercessors have devoured the book *Rees Howells: Intercessor*, which focuses on crisis intervention through intercession during World War II. Mr. Howells had one son, named Samuel, who was given the stewardship of the ministry of the Swansea Bible College in Wales for many years.

Over the years, I have received different assignments from the Lord through dreams and visions. One of these strategic assignments was to re-dig the wells of crisis intercession by praying "on-site with insight" at Rees Howells' home location.

In 1998, I was tremendously privileged to have a personal appointment with Samuel Howells, who was eighty-six years old at the time. Mr. Howells has since gone to be with the Lord, but I still vividly remember sitting in the famous Blue Room where Rees Howells and others interceded during the war. When we moved to another room, a woman came and served us tea and crumpets. She, also, had been involved in the prayer meetings. Samuel Howells was a small, frail man, dressed in a suit and tie. "Wouldn't you like to have another crumpet?" he asked me. At the time, I actually wasn't eating sugar, but I didn't want to offend my host, so I ate several crumpets that day and also drank about four cups of tea.

I asked him, "How did your father receive the revelation of what to pray for during the time of World War II?" I remember being frustrated because he would not answer my questions. Finally, on my knees next to his chair, I prayed to the Lord to give me some way to build a bridge with Mr. Howells. The name Leonard Ravenhill popped into my mind, so I asked, "Did you ever know Leonard Ravenhill?" That seemed to change the atmosphere. He responded, "Oh, yes! Dear Leonard was one of our most favorite guests," and something shifted. I mentioned how I loved his writings, his books, and that I knew his son David.

Then I become bold and asked again, "Did an angel come? Was it dreams or visions? How did your father get his revelations regarding prayer?" And I will never forget how Mr. Howells looked right at me, with tears streaming down his cheeks, and said, "You must understand, the Lord's servant was possessed by God." Then he laid his hands on me and pronounced the mantle of his father, Rees Howells, upon my life. He prayed for me, and in tears and in utter brokenness, he said, "Lord, possess this man. Lord, possess this man." What a glorious day!

That response, "You must understand, the Lord's servant was possessed by God," answered all my questions that day. I did not ask another question. How does revelation come? How does authority over darkness come? How do "breakthroughs" occur? We must understand that the Lord's servants need to be possessed by God!

Since that day, I have almost died four times. And, lately, I've been in so much physical pain that it would be a whole lot easier for me to leave this world. However, I can't, because I have an assignment to fulfill here. It is to help raise up people like you who are possessed by God with a breaker anointing.

I am here to be a bridge from one generation to the next to help carry the cargo from generations past, to help carry it over to the next generation, to tell the old, old stories to create new, new stories of God's majesty and grace.

The gospel is not about Charles Finney, Rees Howells, Rodney Howard-Browne, or Bob Jones. It's about Jesus. God is an equal-opportunity employer!

When Blind Bartimaeus learned that Jesus was coming His way, he cried out with all his heart, *"Jesus, Son of David, have mercy on me!"* (Mark

10:47; Luke 18:38). Today, the Lord is looking for hungry people who will not hold back—those who will cry out with full hearts, "Have mercy upon me, dear Jesus!" We must learn to cast off the cloak of intimidation and whatever else is holding us back, then arise and go to Jesus. He will give us our sight and take possession of us to His glory. Hallelujah!

You qualify as a breaker, a forerunner of revival breakthrough. May the Lord take possession of you in a subtle or dramatic encounter. Your life is not your own. You were bought with a price. Give your all to Him. He has given His all for you. The Lord bless and keep you, my friend.

LET'S PRAY TOGETHER

Gracious Father, we declare that we are not our own; we belong to You, and we are servants of Yours, the Most High God. We are asking, Holy Spirit, that You would descend upon us with a fresh baptism of, and with, the Holy Spirit and fire. Call upon us with a greater and lasting impact. Come and fill us to overflowing. Send us the spirit of intercession for the great harvest. In Jesus's name, come and take possession of us! Thank You, almighty God. Amen and Amen.

9

CLASSIC CHARACTERISTICS OF REVIVAL

"Will You not revive us again,
so that Your people may rejoice in You?"
—Psalm 85:6

This is the last chapter in part 3, "The Power in His Presence." It answers the question "What does true revival look like?" We have previously noted that classic revival goes beyond what we normally consider church "renewal," which impacts the body of Christ but stops short of transforming society. When we consistently seek God's presence and are possessed by Him, He brings radical transformation that spills out from our lives to the world around us.

One of the most famous passages in the entire Bible on revival is Psalm 85, and I have chosen verse 6 for our theme verse: *"Will You not revive us again, so that Your people may rejoice in You?"* Let's pray for God's blessing as we explore the characteristics of true revival, identifying and understanding them so that we can earnestly seek such an awakening in our time.

Father, like the psalmist, we, too, are asking, *"Will You not revive us again?"* You have revived Your people multiple times, and now we ask that You would come again and again and again and again and again, like the waves of the ocean. Let another revival wave roll in, for Jesus Christ's sake. Amen and Amen!

WHAT IS AUTHENTIC REVIVAL?

As I wrote earlier, revival can be defined in a variety of ways because it has multiple features. Here are some definitions that I have gleaned and developed over the years, several of which come from *Webster's* dictionary:

+ Revival is a "return, recall, or recovery to life from death or apparent death; as the revival of a drowned person." Revival is not about something that has never lived at all but about something that was once alive, has died, and has been resurrected. Thus, revival "brings something back to life that is either dead or seemingly dead."

+ Revival brings something back to its earlier state; it is an act of restoration, a return or a recall to activity, like the revival of someone's spirits.

+ Revival is a "recall, return or recovery from a state of neglect, oblivion, obscurity, or depression." Revival restores truth or recalls to obedience that which has been forgotten.

+ Revival is a "renewed and more active attention to religion, an awakening for men to their spiritual concerns." In other words, revival brings a holy shock to apathy and carelessness toward God.

+ Revival counteracts spiritual decline and creates spiritual momentum.

+ Revival brings about the conversion of a large number of people in a relatively short, concentrated period of time.

+ Revival is the spiritual war, or wave, that carries faith from one generation to another.

Next, let's look at some insightful quotes from Christian leaders and authors about the nature of revival:

+ Richard Owen Roberts: "Revival is an extraordinary work of the Holy Spirit producing extraordinary results...the re-entry of Christ's manifest presence."[43]

---

43. Larry Sparks, *Charisma* magazine, "3 Ways to Keep Revival Alive," 2014; https://www.charismamag.com/spirit/revival/19833-3-ways-to-keep-revival-alive.

- Stephen Olford: "Revival is not some emotion or worked-up excitement; it is rather an invasion from heaven which brings a [person] to a conscious awareness of God."[44]

- J. Edwin Orr: "A spiritual awakening is a movement of the Holy Spirit bringing about a revival of New Testament Christianity in the Church of Christ and its related community.... The outpouring of the Spirit accomplishes the reviving of the Church, the awakening of the masses and the movement of uninstructed people toward the Christian faith."[45]

- Charles Finney: The experience of revival is "nothing else than a new beginning of obedience to God...."[46]

- Vance Havner: Revival is a work of "God's Spirit among His own people."[47] "What we call revival is simply New Testament Christianity, the saints getting back to normal."[48]

- A. W. Tozer: "When revival comes it changes the moral climate of a community."[49]

The revived church, by the many or the few, is moved to engage in evangelism, teaching, and social action.

Finally, let me give you a concise statement showing the sequential effects and the momentum of revival:

---

44. Sparks, "3 Ways to Keep Revival Alive."

45. "Revival Summaries—Great Awakenings," *Renewal Journal*, March 10, 2013, https://renewaljournal.com/2013/03/10/great-awakenings/. Incidentally, I obtained the rights to J. Edwin Orr's classic message on revival, and it is transcribed in my book *Prayer Storm* and its corresponding online class.

46. Edgar H. Lewellen, *Revival—God's Proven Method of Awakening His Church* (self-published, 2005), 10, https://books.google.com/books?id=WpDjDx80fzsC&pg=PA10&lpg=PA10&dq=charles+finney+The+experience+of+revival+is+nothing+more+than+a+new+beginning+to+obedience+to+God.

47. Vance Havner, *Hearts Afire*, reprint ed. (Independently published: Solid Christian Books, 2014; Westwood, NJ: Fleming Revell, 1952), 77. Citation refers to the reprint edition.

48. Vance Havner, as quoted in *Spiritual Formation Is...: How to Grow in Jesus with Passion and Confidence* by Rod Dempsey and Dave Earley (Nashville, TN: B&H Academic, 2018), 104.

49. Leonard Ravenhill, "Revival Series, Lecture 1," http://www.ravenhill.org/revival1.htm#:~:text.

Revival is the hunger for change: when revival reaches its fullness, it stirs the individual, which impacts the family, which revives a congregation to spread unity, inspiration, and the fire of God to influence the church in a city or region, which, in turn, releases societal changes before the kingdom of God comes on earth.

We will be expanding on all these ideas in this chapter and throughout the remainder of this book. Carefully reflect on these points and use them as the basis of your prayers because they will be useful as we further explore the characteristics of revival.

PLEAS FOR REVIVAL IN THE BIBLE

Many great pleas for revival are recorded in God's Word, but we will focus here on the three primary Scripture passages that have been used as the basis for prayers by intercessors of genuine revival throughout time.

LORD, *You showed favor to Your land; You restored the fortunes of Jacob. You forgave the guilt of Your people; You covered all their sin. Selah. You withdrew all Your fury; You turned away from Your burning anger. Restore us, God of our salvation, and cause Your indignation toward us to cease. Will You be angry with us forever? Will You prolong Your anger to all generations? Will You not revive us again, so that Your people may rejoice in You?* (Psalm 85:1–6)

LORD, *I have heard the report about You, and I was afraid.* LORD, *revive Your work in the midst of the years, in the midst of the years make it known. In anger remember mercy.* (Habakkuk 3:2)

Oh, that You would tear open the heavens and come down, that the mountains would quake at Your presence—as fire kindles brushwood, as fire causes water to boil—to make Your name known to Your adversaries, that the nations may tremble at Your presence! When You did awesome things which we did not expect, You came down, the mountains quaked at Your presence. For from days of old they have not heard or perceived by ear, nor has the eye seen a God besides You, who acts in behalf of one who waits for Him. (Isaiah 64:1–4)

These Scriptures are excellent to use over and over again, both as a theological foundation for revival and in prayer to move the heart of God and stir your own heart to experience revival breakthrough.

THREE INITIAL STAGES OF REVIVAL

What can we expect as revival unfolds? After spending years studying the subject of revival and going on-site to places of historic revival movements, I have found that there are at least three preliminary stages that lead to an outpouring of the Holy Spirit: (1) an intense hunger for change, (2) prayers to God for change, and (3) networking with other believers toward unity. Let's look at each of these distinct aspects.

1. AN INTENSE HUNGER FOR CHANGE

This is when people are desperate for God and for His transforming power. They recognize the way things should be, but they also have a spiritual revelation and awareness of how terrible the state of things—the condition of one's life, the condition of one's family, city, or nation—currently is. For example, they may have a revelation based on Matthew 5:3 from the Sermon on the Mount: "*Blessed are the poor in spirit, for theirs is the kingdom of heaven.*" In this stage, the people's awareness is, "Oh, how much we need God!" and they begin to seek Him in humility.

Thus, revival is a personal touch in people's hearts concerning spiritual realities, with a strong desire for a change in the status quo. As Matthew 5:6 says, "*Blessed are those who hunger and thirst for righteousness.*" We should note that one of the first signs of physical death is a loss of hunger. When facing death, people lose their desire to eat. In contrast, the first sign of recovery from illness is the request, "Give me something to eat. I'm hungry!"

So, we need to ask ourselves, "How hungry for God am I?"

2. PRAYERS TO GOD FOR CHANGE

Merely a desire for change is not enough. That desire must be channeled through prayer to God, through intercession, which will then be moved toward the next stage of revival breakthrough.[50] When you have a

---

50. To go deeper into this subject, please see my book *Praying with God's Heart* and the corresponding online classes on the purpose and power of prophetic intercession.

deep desire for things to change, either you're going to express that hunger and frustration to God, seeking His guidance and direction, *or* you will become hypercritical toward the church, voicing bitterness, frustration, anger, negativity, and criticism. Eventually, you will withdraw.

How do you usually react to adverse circumstances in your life or troubling issues in society? Do you pour out your heart to God, or do you become angry and criticize? How might God be leading you to intercede today?

3. NETWORKING TOWARD UNITY

Networking to pray and work alongside others to bring revival can sometimes be a simple process, but it has to be very intentional. To even have a desire for these associations, we must understand that we cannot bring about revival breakthrough by ourselves. As Psalm 133:1 says, *"How good and pleasant it is when God's people live together in unity!"* (NIV). Thus, the third step toward revival that puts feet to our hunger and prayers is the relational work of networking, which can result in progressive, joint actions to develop city or regional unity among believers.

We need each other! We need to labor for the bond of unity and peace in the body of Christ. (See Ephesians 4:3; Colossians 3:14.) It takes a citywide church to win a citywide spiritual war. I encourage you to reflect on Jesus's prayer in John 17, which reveals to us His mandate for unity among His disciples.

How are you building bridges with other believers for genuine revival to come?

FIVE CHARACTERISTICS OF REVIVAL

Let us continue to deepen our understanding of the nature of revival by looking at five specific characteristics of classic, historic revivals. Each revival has a distinct and strong characteristic. Yet authentic revival will always include the following elements, which correspond to the traits mentioned above: the church being returned to its original condition as God intended, evangelism and discipleship, and believers being empowered to make positive changes in society.

1. A PASSIONATE DENUNCIATION OF SIN

James 4:4 reminds us that sin is the enemy—not our friend. *"You adulterous people, don't you know that friendship with the world means enmity ["hostility" NASB] against God? Therefore, anyone who chooses to be a friend of the world becomes an enemy of God"* (NIV).

That is straightforward, New Testament apostolic teaching. George Whitefield, an evangelist in the 1700s, preached like a lion, and people were compelled to listen whether they wanted to or not! We, too, need to impress upon people that friendship with the world is hostility toward God. In today's hyper-grace culture, people are often tagged as having "a religious spirit" if their preaching or discussions about sin are too candid. But the passionate denunciation of sin is one of the characteristics of revival.

Of course, an outpouring of the grace of God is also a necessary quality of authentic moves of the Holy Spirit. Otherwise, people's response to the call may be (or turn into) a mere legalistic adherence to God's commands. But when there is a *passionate pursuit of the character of God* that is *empowered by grace*, it produces transformation. "Holy violence"—an intensity in the call for repentance and a fervent, passionate response to that call—was often a trait of historic moves of God's presence. Thus, among the classic characteristics of revival, we see people deeply repenting of their sin and coming forward to receive God's grace.

2. A REVELATION OF GOD'S HOLINESS

First Peter 1:16 says, *"You shall be holy, for I am holy."* In the 1700s, Jonathan Edwards preached under this conviction. Many other revivalists have done so, as well, including Leonard Ravenhill, a famed British evangelist and the author of *Why Revival Tarries*, whom I had the pleasure of knowing.

It was said that Edwards was consumed with an awful awareness of the holiness of God, not wanting to do anything that would displease the Lord. Again, I understand there could be a danger of falling into legalism if a response to the call for holiness is not grace empowered. However, I am speaking here of a *revelation* of God's holiness, not merely an understanding of the *doctrine* of divine holiness.

Earlier, I mentioned a vision I received in which I ascended a ladder and had a revelation of God's beauty. All I saw was light that exposed and dispelled every level of darkness, and I just kept declaring, "You're beautiful!" That's a revelation of God's holiness, and it draws us to Him, not away from Him. His holiness is beautiful. It truly is.

3. A DEEP AWARENESS OF THE LOVE AND MERCY OF GOD

If I were listing these characteristics sequentially, perhaps this quality would be number one. But if I were to do so, it could make the characteristics into a mathematical equation, and that they are not. These components must be Holy Spirit directed, grace empowered, and relationally motivated. Romans 8:35–39 encourages us with these words:

> *Who will separate us from the love of Christ? Will tribulation, or trouble, or persecution, or famine, or nakedness, or danger, or sword? Just as it is written: "For Your sake we are killed all day long; we were regarded as sheep to be slaughtered." But in all these things we overwhelmingly conquer through Him who loved us. For I am convinced that neither death, nor life, nor angels, nor principalities, nor things present, nor things to come, nor powers, nor height, nor depth, nor any other created thing will be able to separate us from the love of God that is in Christ Jesus our Lord.*

It was said of St. Francis of Assisi, as well as the protestant Bible teacher-evangelist D. L. Moody, that they only preached about the love of God. Can you imagine that? Their only topic was God's love and compassion. Amazing. As it says in Romans 2:4, the loving-kindness of God draws us to repentance.

I love reading about the life of David Brainerd, a missionary to the First Nations people of America. He would stand in the cold, in the snow, and preach with conviction the love of God, the Messiah, the Lord Jesus Christ. He would tell them that the Lord Jesus was a kind and compassionate Master to the First Nations people. He would be moved upon with deep spiritual distress, pleading with tears for the people to accept the everlasting mercy of God.

If we do not know and express the love of God, revival has not yet come to us. Let us keep these familiar but revolutionary words of Jesus continually alive in our hearts:

> For God **so loved the world**, that He gave His only Son, so that everyone who believes in Him will not perish, but have eternal life.
> (John 3:16)

> By this all people will know that you are My disciples: if you **have love for one another**.
> (John 13:35)

4. A HEIGHTENED CONSCIOUSNESS OF ETERNITY

I currently attend a charismatic-style, Spirit-filled, evangelical church, and this church is the first one I have attended in well over thirty years that presents at least a three- to five-minute gospel presentation at the end of every message, giving people an opportunity to accept Jesus as their Lord and Savior. The leaders of the church do not assume that everybody in the house is walking with Jesus. Some people may know about religion, but perhaps they don't yet have a relationship with the Lord. As a result of this practice of regularly presenting the gospel, I have witnessed with my own eyes more people come to faith in the past five years than I have seen in a church in more than two decades. The basic reason for this is that these presentations help to bring people a heightened consciousness of eternity and their need for a Savior.

Similarly, one time, I was ministering in Argentina, and I was absolutely fascinated by one church's service, which actually included five-minute segments *during* the message when an evangelist would get up and share the gospel. There would be an invitation to accept Christ right then, and when people would come forward to receive the Lord Jesus, they would be taken aside, welcomed into God's family, and offered counsel and prayer. I thought that was a wonderful, novel idea. It keeps eternal matters in the forefront of people's minds.

Thus, in classic revival, the reality of heaven and hell are preached, with an appeal to the lost to come to God to be saved. Can you tell me the last time you heard a teaching in church on the topic of hell? You probably can't. You know what? That's sad, and it's one of the reasons why we don't often experience true, authentic revival. If they don't hear preaching or teaching about eternity, most people will not develop a deep-felt need for salvation.

Consider some of Jonathan Edwards's intense sermon titles: "Sinners in the Hands of an Angry God," "Wrath Upon the Wicked to the Uttermost," and "Eternity of Hell's Torments." Do we truly understand that there is a real heaven and a real hell? Revelation 20:11–15 describes this reality as follows:

> Then I saw a great white throne and him who was seated on it. The earth and the heavens fled from his presence, and there was no place for them. And I saw the dead, great and small, standing before the throne, and books were opened. Another book was opened, which is the book of life. The dead were judged according to what they had done as recorded in the books. The sea gave up the dead that were in it, and death and Hades gave up the dead that were in them, and each person was judged according to what they had done. Then death and Hades were thrown into the lake of fire. The lake of fire is the second death. Anyone whose name was not found written in the book of life was thrown into the lake of fire.
>
> (NIV)

Today, we need to return to the revelation of the eternal judgment of God and the reality of heaven and hell.[51] One of my goals is to compose a series called "Eternity" about this very topic.

One time, I was praying over a man, and I gave him this word: "You're going to hell." Well, that was a good word to say to someone, wasn't it? I actually said, "You're going to hell" twenty-three times. My words were even recorded. Well, the man was subsequently in a car accident, and he did indeed visit hell. He was in hell for twenty-three minutes but came back. He was a believer, but he went to hell. Afterward, he wrote a book

---

51. For more on this subject, please see my book *A Radical Faith* (Franklin, TN: God Encounters Ministries, 2020), and its corresponding online classes, in which I teach about the resurrection of the dead and eternal judgment.

about it entitled *23 Minutes in Hell*,[52] which was later made into a movie. The man's wife wrote me a letter and sent a gift to my ministry, and she and her husband have the recording of my prophecy that he was going to go to hell.

In revival, God calls us to face reality—eternal reality.

5. EXPERIENTIAL CONVICTION OF SIN

Genuine conviction of sin is another sign of true revival. John 16:7–8 says, *"But I tell you the truth: it is to your advantage that I am leaving; for if I do not leave, the Helper will not come to you; but if I go, I will send Him to you. **And He, when He comes, will convict the world regarding sin**, and righteousness, and judgment."* One of the primary ministries of Holy Spirit is to convict people of the state of their lives and their need for God.

Convicting the world concerning sin, righteousness, and judgment ties into people's conscious awareness of eternity and the judgment to come. Such conviction is God's job, and it is part of the amazing work of the Holy Spirit. He convicts or convinces human beings of their sinful condition and need for righteousness, as well as the reality that we will each stand before the judgment seat of Christ. (See, for example, 2 Corinthians 5:10.)

Perhaps the move of God that we desperately need will return when the Holy Spirit comes to us anew with conviction. A scoffer of George Whitefield was quoted as saying, "I came to hear you with my pocket full of stones, intending to break your head; but your sermon got the better of me, and broke my heart."[53]

Once again, we need a pure move of God like what occurred in 1790–1800, in the rough frontier of Kentucky, when people would cry out for mercy when experiential conviction fell upon them.

Or in the United Kingdom in 1859, when it is said that men staggered down due to the wounds to their consciences.

---

52. Bill Wiese, *23 Minutes in Hell*, 10th anniversary edition (Lake Mary, FL: Charisma House, 2017).
53. J. C. Ryle, "J. C. Ryle's Estimation of Whitefield's Ministry," Grace Online Library, https://graceonlinelibrary.org/biographies/j-c-ryles-estimation-of-whitefields-ministry-by-j-c-ryle/.

Or in the Hebrides Island Revival, when there was a five-mile zone where people would come into an open portal, an open heaven, and be convicted of sin. Some people turned themselves in to the police department to make amends for past wrongs.

We need the Spirit of conviction of sin and mercy through Christ. Let us echo the prayer of Evan Roberts of the Welsh revival: "Send Your Spirit now, more powerfully, for Jesus Christ's sake. Amen!"

OUR NECESSARY RESPONSES

How should we respond to the powerful characteristics of revival we have covered in this chapter? I urge you to respond in the following ways:

PRAY!

We need to respond with prayer, which is the appropriate application. Remember, when faced with difficult circumstances and dire societal needs, we may be tempted to respond with frustration and anger, but we must take our deep concerns to the heavenly Father. Extreme times take extreme measures, and desperate circumstances require desperate responses. This is the hour for prayer. A great worldwide prayer movement continues to grow. May the Holy Spirit grip us until we are consumed with the zeal of the Lord, as Jesus was, for the Father's house to become *"a house of prayer for all the nations"* (Mark 11:17).

TAKE BOLD ACTION

I mentioned earlier that we must add feet to our faith. It is not enough to be a prayer warrior alone. We need not only prayer, but also personal action and boldness. In this way, we may often be the answer to our own prayers. Proverbs 28:1 says, *"The righteous are as bold as a lion"* (NIV). And as C. S. Lewis stated in The Chronicles of Narnia, "Aslan is not a tame lion." Jesus our Messiah is not only the Lamb of God, but He is also the Lion of the Tribe of Judah. For instance, He made bold statements that a primary sign of those who belong to Him is that they care for the needs of others in tangible ways. (See, for example, Matthew 25:31–46.)

RECEIVE A REALITY CHECK

We must also understand that if we really put our hand to the plow of revival, we will experience persecution. All revivals in the past were criticized and attacked. No advance of the kingdom goes unchallenged. What you challenge will challenge you back. If you "target" individuals for revival, persecution will come from individuals. If you target the church for awakening, persecution will come from the church. If you target society for spiritual transformation, segments of society will target you back.

But remember, we can't turn back from the call. We must pick up the baton of revival in our day and in our time. We must pick up our cross and continue the journey toward unprecedented conversions, resulting in fervent congregations walking together in the love of God—impacting society and declaring and demonstrating that, indeed, Jesus Christ is Lord of all!

THE GREATER-WORKS GENERATION

Let the cry arise and the fullness of the Holy Spirit take hold in our lives. Not only do we need a return of the convicting work of Holy Spirit, but we also need to embrace His power, as declared in Acts 1:8: *"You will receive power when the Holy Spirit has come upon you; and you shall be My witnesses both in Jerusalem and in all Judea, and Samaria, and as far as the remotest part of the earth."*

How can we be part of the greater-works generation that Jesus declared was coming? (See John 14:12.) We must receive the power of the spiritual gifts, including the gifts of healings, faith, and the workings of miracles. Long-term transformation transpires in the life of an individual, a church, a city, a society, or a culture only by the dynamic power of the Holy Spirit. We require the three-cord strand of the fullness of fruit, power, and wisdom brought together for such a time as this![54]

---

54. See my books *Passionate Pursuit* (New Kensington, PA: Whitaker House, 2015) and *Releasing Spiritual Gifts Today* (New Kensington, PA: Whitaker House, 2016) for teachings on the power of the Holy Spirit.

LET'S PRAY TOGETHER

Glorious Father God, we need a radical restoration of the fruit, gifts, and wisdom of the Holy Spirit in our day. Give us revelation about the realities of heaven and hell. Restore to us the classic characteristics of revival, including the experiential conviction of sin and the necessity of living holy lives. Send us even more of the power of Your Holy Spirit. Release an outbreak of signs and wonders and miracles. According to Psalm 85, according to Hosea, according to Habakkuk, and according to Isaiah, revive us again! We thank You and praise You, in Jesus's great name. Amen and Amen.

PART FOUR:

THE GREAT HARVEST

10

REVIVAL MANIFESTATIONS
AND PHENOMENA

*"Call to Me and I will answer you, and I will tell you great and
mighty things, which you do not know."*
—Jeremiah 33:3

Now we begin part 4 of this book, "The Great Harvest." I have spent
many, many hours preparing, working on, praying over, chewing on, studying, adding to, deleting from, and praying some more over this chapter,
because I want it to be presented well as a blessing to you.

We have already explored characteristics of revival, so now we will look
at other activity that is often a part of, or associated with, the culture of
revival. Revivals often come with some unusual manifestations—at least
they seem unusual to most people. Therefore, I felt it would be beneficial
to help prepare you for manifestations and phenomena that may become
apparent during your journey toward revival breakthrough. As you exercise discernment, be open to receive all that God has for you.

Let's pray together that you may better understand and receive the
wonders of God in revival:

Father, thank You so much for this opportunity to be led by Your Spirit as we explore what You would have us to learn. We are very grateful that You are leading the way. We are thankful that rejoicing in You will be part of the manifestation of revival: a great rejoicing will break out as we glorify Your name! Amen and Amen.

To give a brief review, "revival" is often defined as a season of powerful visitation from God that includes the presence of the Holy Spirit made manifest and often tangible. It is true that God is always with us, but there are certain times when it is as if God breaks through time, waves His hand, and says to us, "I'm here!" That's what happens in a revival or an awakening. The Lord shows up and manifests Himself in a way people can clearly recognize—visually, audibly, or otherwise. During such a time, the church is restored to life, and believers walk in the Lord Jesus Christ with a renewed love and passion for Him.

The development of terminology that describes and defines revival characteristics is a major part of church history. We can identify very specific common and dominant characteristics that have occurred during historic revivals. These characteristics center on God's acting to strengthen the church through powerful manifestations of His presence. Such manifestations in revival thrust believers to go forth and awaken society at large to spiritual matters, as the power of the Holy Spirit permeates their lives and even the atmosphere around them.

A good example of a common characteristic is being "possessed by God," a quality I described earlier. Other distinct features of revival include the conviction of sin, a revelation of eternity, a sense of the enormity of God's great love, powerful conversions, supernatural encounters, spiritual fervor, and lasting spiritual fruit resulting in a legacy for the church. The ultimate quality of revival is wide-scale cultural change, with numerous people coming to accept Jesus as their Lord and Savior and having their lives transformed.

Let us now examine more closely some particular revival manifestations, some of which we have already briefly covered. Focusing on them together will help us to gain a greater understanding of what to expect as God powerfully moves in our midst.

INTENSITY OF EMOTION IN CONVERSION

In revival, the usual biblical elements of conversion are present among people, such as repentance and a sense of joy as a result of being reconciled to the Lord. However, these experiences are often heightened and intensified. It is as if people are looking through a magnifying glass, and the revelations and experiences they receive appear up close and vivid.

This intensity is reflected in the way the newly converted ones express themselves. For example, sometimes, when people are saved in revival, they will be exuberant with joy. Certain people will connect immediately with such passionate joy, while others won't. But expect that some individuals will not be able to hold back from praising God. And there is no reason for them to try to hold back, because "they once were blind, but now they can see"! (See John 9:25.)

In revival history, a number of people have first manifested deep sorrow for wrongdoing, weeping over their sinful conditions as a result of being convicted, and then repenting of their sins. Their agony and travail under conviction have been followed by periods of extreme, overwhelming joy because they know in their hearts that they have been forgiven.

For example, I previously mentioned the sermon titles of Jonathan Edwards, one of the great preachers of the First Great Awakening in the 1700s. It is said that under Edwards's anointed words, while he preached the sermon "Sinners in the Hands of an Angry God" to a congregation in Enfield, Connecticut, some people were so gripped by the realities of eternity that they grabbed hold of the backs of the pews in front of them to keep from "sliding into hell"—the sense of spiritual danger felt so real to them. Edwards's theme for that sermon was Deuteronomy 32:35: *"Their foot shall slide in due time: for the day of their calamity is at hand, and the things that shall come upon them make haste"* (KJV).[55] As Edwards preached this sermon and others, people experienced great agony followed by great ecstasy.

We may expect similar intensity of emotion in contemporary revival as people respond to the convicting work of the Spirit.

---

55. Jonathan Edwards, "Sinners in the Hands of an Angry God," sermon at Enfield, CT, July 8, 1741, https://www.ccel.org/e/edwards/sermons/sinners.html; accessed February 5, 2021.

EMPOWERING GIFTS OF THE HOLY SPIRIT[56]

Among other revival phenomena is an outpouring of spiritual gifts. Prophecy, healings, and miracles have been features of many great revivals throughout the centuries. Revival history is like the waves of the ocean, where one wave is followed by another wave, and ensuing moves of the Holy Spirit build upon the previous ones. The present-day movements of God in the United States and beyond are an overflow of the Pentecostal Azusa Street Revival, which occurred during the early 1900s in Los Angeles, California.

Each subsequent expression has included the empowerment of the gifts of the Holy Spirit as an essential feature of the revival. The following is a brief overview of some of these waves of the Holy Spirit:

+ 1920s: The Healing Revival

+ 1948: The Latter Rain Movement/Healing Deliverance campaigns

+ 1950s: The Evangelical thrust

+ 1960s: The Charismatic, Jesus People, and Messianic movements

+ 1980s: The Third Wave and the Global Prayer movements

+ 1988: The Prophetic emergence

+ 1990s: The Toronto Blessing and the Brownsville Revival

+ 2000s: The Apostolic Reformation

According to Hebrews 13:8, *"Jesus Christ is the same yesterday and today, and forever."* What He has done before, He will do today! Let us expect an outpouring of the gifts of the Spirit.

SIGNS AND WONDERS

Manifestations of revival have also included signs and wonders. The crusades of evangelists such as Kathryn Kuhlman included healings and miracles. Yet what the world needs now are not just a few highly gifted people but the full restoration of the fivefold gifts and ministries of the

---

56. For an in-depth study on manifestations and phenomena that occur in revival, please see my online classes "Releasing Spiritual Gifts Today" and "Walking in the Supernatural Life."

Holy Spirit, which equip *every* believer to do *"greater works"* (John 14:12) for God's kingdom. What are these fivefold gifts and ministries?

> *And He gave some as **apostles**, some as **prophets**, some as **evangelists**, some as **pastors** and **teachers**, for the equipping of the saints for the work of ministry, for the building up of the body of Christ; until we all attain to the unity of the faith, and of the knowledge of the Son of God, to a mature man, to the measure of the stature which belongs to the fullness of Christ.* (Ephesians 4:11–13)

The restoration of the fivefold gifts is often associated with revival, reformation, and awakenings, and this restoration leads to the manifestation of signs and wonders. Such visible, supernatural phenomena point to the invisible spiritual activity of God. They correspond to the manifestation experienced by Jesus's disciples on the day of Pentecost. In Acts 2, the Holy Spirit arrived with the sound of a mighty rushing wind and the appearance of flames of fire, accompanied by the release of the gift of tongues as an outward, visible sign pointing to an inward spiritual reality. These manifestations were signs of the coming of the Holy Spirit, and they attested to the death, resurrection, and ascension of the Lord Jesus Christ.

Let's be expectant about seeing signs and wonders in our time! Jesus declared, *"And **these signs** [manifestations and phenomena] **will follow those who believe**: in My name they will cast out demons; they will speak with new tongues"* (Mark 16:17 NKJV). Signs follow believers who exercise their faith in God.

Over the years, I've seen many signs and wonders. I have seen the gifts of healings in operation in so many diverse ways that I've had to throw away the cookie cutter. We can't follow a formula because God may manifest His presence and power in new and unexpected ways.

In Ephesians 1:18–20, we read:

> *I pray that the eyes of your heart may be enlightened, so that you will know…what is the **boundless greatness of His power toward us who believe**. These are in accordance with the working of the strength of His might which He brought about in Christ, when He raised Him from the dead and seated Him at His right hand in the heavenly places….*

In this passage, the Greek word translated *"working"* is *energeia*, which can signify "effectual working."[57] *Energeia* is the effectual empowering of the Holy Spirit. God's diverse power at work within us is absolutely amazing—and sometimes unexpected. For example, one day I was out doing routine errands, picking up dry cleaning, mailing a package to my son for his birthday, things like that. At the UPS store, a man came over to me and said, "Wait, wait, I know your voice. You're that guy!" He added, "I was listening online a couple of nights ago, and I stumbled onto a podcast…. Because of you, I got delivered from an evil spirit!"

Why am I telling you this story? I want you to understand that such outcomes are not about me—how I look or how I sound. This deliverance happened because *signs follow those who believe*. Signs are *supposed* to follow us. God wants His children's "shadows" to fall on people, bringing healing and freedom. (See Acts 5:15–16.) The Lord wants signs and wonders to happen through your life, bringing Him glory.

I hope you realize that "revival time" is not limited to the times when we are in church meetings or attending Bible studies or taking online classes for spiritual training. Revival is supposed to be happening in everyday life—when you're at the grocery store or the gas station, whatever you're doing and wherever you are.

THE SIGNIFICANCE OF MANIFESTATIONS

When we encounter a supernatural phenomenon in revival, there are various aspects to consider.

IS IT FROM GOD?

The first question we should ask is, "Is this manifestation from God?" To help answer this question, it may be possible to trace some prophetic symbolism in the manifestations and the phenomena themselves. We need to seek the Lord about the significance of His plan for revival, restoration, and the end times.

Too often, people interpret divine signs as being mindless excesses or dangerous sidetracks. They may even construe a supernatural element as

---

57. *Strong's Exhaustive Concordance of the Bible*, #G1753, electronic version, © 1980, 1986, and assigned to World Bible Publishers, Inc. Used by permission. All rights reserved.

a demonic counterfeit. As we will discuss in more detail later in this chapter, we need to rely on the Bible as our source of truth to verify whether a particular phenomenon is genuine. We should also look to precedence in church history to determine if a manifestation has stood the test of time and the scrutiny of wise church leaders.

The devil may try to fool us with false manifestations. Besides that, some people may effect various manifestations because they want to draw attention to themselves. However, their fabricated behavior does not invalidate authentic phenomena from God. If we seek God first in all things, He will be faithful to respond to our questions about which spiritual expressions are valid.

Revival phenomena have manifested since the day of Pentecost, but the Bible predicts that, in the last-days outpouring, they are going to increase. Are such phenomena biblical? Are they of God? Or are they contrary to God and His Word? Here is the bottom line: if they're not of God, we don't want them. If they are of God, we want them because we need to know what God is doing in them, through them, and alongside them. We can't afford to miss what God is doing just because we don't understand it.

WHAT DOES IT MEAN?

Manifestations of revival such as intensity in conversion, the outpouring of the gifts of the Holy Spirit, and the demonstration of signs and wonders are significant, but you may wonder about the actual purpose of many of them. On the day of Pentecost, people had the same question when they heard the believers speaking in tongues:

> Utterly amazed, they asked: "Aren't all these who are speaking Galileans? Then how is it that each of us hears them in our native language?... (Both Jews and converts to Judaism); Cretans and Arabs—we hear them declaring the wonders of God in our own tongues!" Amazed and perplexed, they asked one another, "What does this mean?"
> (Acts 2:7–8, 11–12 NIV)

"What does this phenomenon mean?" is a question we should ask as well. On the day of Pentecost, Peter explained to the people that the sign of tongues signified the outpouring of the Holy Spirit as promised by the prophet Joel. Again, it was also a sign of God's confirmation of Jesus's life, ministry, death, and resurrection. And it announced a time of God's visitation, which the people needed to respond to in order to receive salvation.

Signs similar to that of the tongues of fire on Pentecost have happened in modern times as well. I have a photo of my late wife, Michal Ann, ministering in Mozambique. In that picture, as she is speaking to the crowd before her, fire like that of Acts chapter 2 can be seen "sitting" on people's heads. I've been in other meetings and gatherings where I have seen fire fall on people like that, and they have been set free from demonic affliction and cleansed by the sanctifying work of the Holy Spirit.

Signs and wonders *will* follow those who believe. I know this for certain. What do these signs and wonders mean? For the answers, we need to seek God in each instance. In the above example about my own experience, the fire of God falling on people was to indicate that the Holy Spirit was present to cleanse, set free, and empower!

IS THERE A HUMAN ELEMENT INVOLVED?

Can a revival phenomenon be a human physical reaction and/or a human emotional response to how the Holy Spirit is working, *along with* a Holy Spirit manifestation? Yes. Remember what Charles Finney wrote about being filled with the Holy Spirit:

> The Holy Spirit descended upon me in a manner that seemed to go through me, body and soul. I could feel the impression, like a wave of electricity, going through and through me. Indeed it seemed to come in waves, and waves of liquid love—for I could not express it in any other way.[58]

When the Holy Spirit is empowering, energizing, and manifesting within us, our human bodies, in their frail capacity, may react physically and/or emotionally. How various people have reacted to God's powerful presence has been well-documented throughout revival history. Manifestations that are happening today have occurred before with remarkable similarity.

---

58. Finney, *Memoirs*.

Dr. Martyn Lloyd-Jones was one of the most brilliant and logical theologians of modern times. In his renowned book *Revival*, he says that we ought to expect physical and emotional manifestations or effects as human reactions to God's power because of the very nature of our human constitution. He warns against rejecting the expression of such manifestations:

> Let us be very careful that we do not do violence to man's very nature and constitution. Man reacts as a whole. And it is just folly to expect that he can react in the realm of the spiritual without anything at all happening to the rest of him, to the soul, and to the body.
>
> And so we must expect this kind of reaction in a period of revival, and we must expect different people to react in different ways.[59]

When they see individuals responding emotionally to the work of the Holy Spirit in revival, some people say, "Yeah, but that behavior is just 'soulish,'" as if the soul is fleshly or satanic. The soul is not fleshly or devilish; the soul is God-given. Human beings have a spirit, a body, *and* a soul, with the soul being composed of the mind, the will, and the emotions.

Why am I placing an emphasis on physical and emotional manifestations during revival? As I wrote at the beginning of this chapter, if you're going to embrace a revival culture, you have to be prepared for it. When people are saved and delivered, they may react in physical ways or openly display their emotions. You might just hear a shout or two!

Let me share a personal story that I hope will help you to be prepared for the unexpected. One time, when I was praying for a man to be delivered, the Holy Spirit showed up in power. I knew what the demonic hindrance was, and I was calling forth a greater release of the presence and power of Holy Spirit and angelic assistance for the man. And as I "leaned in" for this greater release of power, a sound like that of a freight train roared out of the man's mouth, and he was delivered from a dominating, manipulative, Jezebel spirit of witchcraft. Such manifestations can happen when the power of the Holy Spirit shows up because a collision between spiritual forces is taking place. God's Spirit is driving out the kingdom of darkness.

---

59. Martyn Lloyd-Jones, *Revival* (Wheaton, IL: Crossway, 1987), 145.

MISTAKES OR "DITCHES" TO AVOID

As we experience and/or observe revival phenomena, we need to avoid three major mistakes or "ditches": (1) becoming sidetracked, (2) developing an attitude of "having arrived," and (3) being offended by certain manifestations.

1. BECOMING SIDETRACKED

We can become sidetracked by focusing exclusively on revival manifestations, as if the phenomena were the essence of revival itself or the goal of what God was doing. This pitfall happened to some people who examined the gifts of the Spirit that accompanied the birth of the Pentecostal Movement at the turn of the twentieth century, and to others who examined the Charismatic Renewal of the 1960s. Sometimes the critics of the gifts forced those who had experienced them to be on the defensive. These critics could hardly stop talking about the gifts in their attempt to discredit them. As a result, believers in these movements spent too much time justifying the gifts rather than constructively developing and shaping the use of these gifts to build up the body of Christ.

Like the gifts of the Spirit, the current phenomena we are experiencing in portions of the church can be defined and defended. Yet, in the process of doing so, we must guard against the tendency to become so preoccupied with our examinations and justifications that we miss the overall purpose of these wonders from the Lord. Spiritual gifts are tools for a spiritual work beyond their mere presence or exercise. The current phenomena should be seen as by-products of something greater and therefore as signs pointing beyond themselves to the presence and activity of almighty God.

2. DEVELOPING AN ATTITUDE OF "HAVING ARRIVED"

Another danger of focusing on the phenomena is in conveying the impression that, if you exhibit these manifestations, you have spiritually "arrived." If we harbor such an attitude, we can develop arrogance or pride that leads us to believe we are better than others.

Even realizing this danger, I still find it very beneficial to welcome the Holy Spirit in whatever manner He chooses to come. Unusual hallmarks of the Holy Spirit could well be preparations for authentic revival, the beginning of something greater coming from heaven to earth. Remember, our primary message is not the presence of such manifestations as "gold dust" or "heavenly feathers," or even the appearance of God's greater glory. It is God Himself. Our message is the God of glory and the God of encounters. Authentic signs must point to the message that leads to the Messenger—Christ Jesus. Let's keep our focus on God!

3. BEING OFFENDED BY CERTAIN MANIFESTATIONS

Many people regard revival manifestations as offensive; it is their main justification for rejecting the present-day activity of the Holy Spirit. But as the saying goes, "God offends the mind to reveal the heart." We need to examine our hearts to avoid becoming offended at what God is doing in renewal and revival.

There are various reasons people may become offended by manifestations. Such phenomena might not fit into the current parameters of their theology. If our theology has no place for revival or the phenomena that accompanies it, then we need a new theology! If our "orthodoxy" squeezes out the Holy Spirit, it is not true orthodoxy. Disruptive events and changed circumstances in society have often driven God's people back to the Bible as their source for values, belief systems, and theology in line with how the Lord is working in their day.

Other people may adhere to a contemporary philosophical approach that examines the nature of religious and spiritual experiences from a biased lens. That lens might be a Western mindset that has been dominated or influenced by the following worldviews:

+ Rationalism, one definition of which is "reliance on reason as the basis for establishment of religious truth"[60]

+ Philosophical materialism: the belief that matter is all that exists or all that is important

+ The Greek concept of a dualism of spirit and matter; this is the idea that the spirit realm does not readily interact with the material world

---

60. *Merriam-Webster.com Dictionary*, s.v. "rationalism," https://www.merriam-webster.com/dictionary/rationalism.

+ Deism: the notion that God the Creator set up world and then left it to run itself without any intervention from Him

Perhaps as a reaction to these Western mindsets, there is also unfortunately a growing influence and practice of mysticism and new age ideas in our culture. In some of these practices, the mind is "blanked out" and/or rejected. People who espouse these ideas may be open to certain spiritual phenomena, but they lack a biblical understanding of true spirituality; they don't seem to realize that God has given human beings a spirit, a soul, and a body, and that each of these areas is to be valued and used.

The extent to which we embrace the various philosophical and spiritual influences outlined above will affect the way in which we view revival phenomena. Many of us are not aware of our philosophical and cultural preconditioning and how this may color our theological perspectives.

There may also be psychological factors at work. We are often not aware of how our own psychological makeup can affect how we react to revival phenomena, both in our own lives and in the lives of others. Psychologists often find religious phenomena an extremely interesting field of study. They may assume that there are psychological explanations for everything from conversion to speaking in tongues, not to mention manifestations such as shaking, laughing, and falling.

As mentioned earlier, human factors can sometimes be at play in revival phenomena. Taking that aspect into consideration can help us to understand human reactions to manifestations under certain circumstances. Likewise, it can be helpful for us to note similarities in religious phenomena that occur in different religions and cultures around the world as a reason why some people may be skeptical about revival manifestations.

However, we must remember that the enemy of darkness is a fake and a copycat. And psychological explanations for some people's reactions do not validate false conclusions about authentic spiritual experiences.

Having examined the various arguments that opponents have presented to revival manifestations, it is my view that when it really comes down to it, the people who reject what the Spirit is doing today do so primarily because they can't accept certain manifestations or phenomena.

They do not like "the mess" that comes along with the package of God's visitation.

In reality, none of us does. But it is as though we feel that God needs our permission to act in a certain way. Well, He doesn't! As I expressed earlier, although we are gatekeepers of His presence, *He is not the guest of the house. He owns the house* and is ultimately in charge of the operation of the manifestations of the Holy Spirit. Therefore, in revival, we continually need to ask ourselves, "Am I offended at God's present work in my life or in others' lives?" If we are, we can seek the Lord and ask Him to help us to be open to the movements of His Spirit.

PROPERLY DISCERNING REVIVAL PHENOMENA

The main issue in either accepting or rejecting manifestations is to properly discern the phenomena. As John wrote:

> *Beloved, do not believe every spirit, but test the spirits to see whether they are from God.* (1 John 4:1)

We need to study and test the spirits. Always look to the Lord and trust that He will show you which manifestations are genuinely from Him.

IS IT BIBLICAL?

The living Word of God is always our final authority in such matters. The Bible is dynamic, not just in relation to the historical contexts of its books, but also in its ability to authoritatively speak to people in every period of history, including our own. The Holy Spirit is the Author of the Scriptures, and He communicates to us today through the Bible:

> *For the word of God is living and powerful, and sharper than any two-edged sword, piercing even to the division of soul and spirit, and of joints and marrow, and is **a discerner of the thoughts and intents of the heart**.* (Hebrews 4:12 NKJV)

> *From childhood you have known the sacred writings which are able to **give you the wisdom** that leads to salvation through faith which is in Christ Jesus. **All Scripture is inspired by God and beneficial for***

*teaching, for rebuke, for correction, for training in righteousness; so that the man or woman of God may be **fully capable, equipped for every good work.*** (2 Timothy 3:15–17)

The Bible is a sufficient Sourcebook for all aspects of our relationship with God, for all time. Paul wrote to Timothy that the Scriptures are able to give us *"wisdom that leads to salvation."* I believe this word *"salvation"* applies to all of God's saving work in the world. But to gain this wisdom, we must first be diligent to study God's Word: *"Be diligent to present yourself approved to God as a worker who does not need to be ashamed, accurately handling the word of truth"* (2 Timothy 2:15).

SCRIPTURAL PRECEDENTS

The initial test to determine if a manifestation is biblical is to look for precedents or examples of that manifestation in Scripture. The biblical record shows many people having powerful encounters with God, often with evident physical and emotional effects. These effects are remarkably similar to those experienced by people in the revivals of church history and in today's moves of the Spirit. That is why a biblical study of physical effects can be fruitful.

SCRIPTURAL PRINCIPLES

If there are no such precedents for a particular manifestation, we need to ask: "Is the phenomenon consistent with biblical principles?" I think this question touches on the most basic consideration of all. If there are clear biblical examples, the situation is relatively easy. But even if there are no biblical examples of something, it does not mean it is unbiblical, as long as it is consistent with principles drawn from the revelation of Scripture. It would be nonsense to expect there to be specific scriptural examples for everything that we do in our lives and relationships with God. To have such a mindset is to misunderstand the nature of the Bible itself.

To use the illustration of prayer, the Bible does not record, by precept or by exact example, every prayer we will ever need to pray on every single occasion. However, we do have as our model the Lord's Prayer, which consists of six short petitions that point to principles that guide and govern our praying at all times. Its themes cover virtually every need we will ever have. We are to apply the principles of prayer to our personal or corporate situations as the Holy Spirit illuminates and enables us.

Of course, we must also carefully examine the question, "Are there any biblical reasons why a particular manifestation may *not* be of God?" Some examples would be if a phenomenon glorifies people rather than the Lord, or if it pulls people down in fear or discouragement rather than lifts them up to the Lord. I discuss this question further in the section "Are the Fruits Good?"

ARE WE LISTENING TO BOTH WORD AND SPIRIT?

The Word of God has a unique relationship with the Spirit of God. There is no competition between them; rather, they are in divine cooperation with one another. Acts 13:1 describes, *"Now there were prophets and teachers at Antioch, in the church that was there."* Here we see a blend of prophecy, revelation, and teaching contributing to the life of the church. In the New Testament, the Holy Spirit illuminated believers' minds to the truths of the Scriptures and to God's will.

The Word of God cannot be fully understood merely according to the grammatical, historical, and theological principles of hermeneutics. These are essential foundations of biblical interpretation, but, as Jesus suggests in His criticism of the Sadducean approach to doctrine, they are inadequate by themselves. *"Jesus answered and said to them, 'You are mistaken, since you do not understand the Scriptures nor the power of God'"* (Matthew 22:29).

Jesus exposed the Sadducees' error: an inadequate understanding of the power and majesty of God. This erroneous mindset kept them locked into a religious system of interpretation of Scripture. Their approach robbed them of a potential vital relationship with God and access to dynamic applications of the truths in His Word.

Thus, while we always look to the Word, we also look to the present illumination of the Holy Spirit. The apostle Paul understood the necessity of our receiving revelation by the Holy Spirit in order to grasp a proper interpretation of spiritual truths. He emphasized this point in Ephesians 1:17–18:

That the God of our Lord Jesus Christ, the Father of glory, may give to you the spirit of wisdom and revelation in the knowledge of Him, the eyes of your understanding being enlightened; that you may know what is the hope of His calling, what are the riches of the glory of His inheritance in the saints.

If this blended model of the established Word of God and the revelation of the Spirit was effective for Jesus, Paul, and the church at Ephesus, then it is the model for us today as well.

IS IT BIBLICALLY ALLOWABLE *OR BIBLICALLY* NECESSARY?

There is a subtle but far-reaching distinction that must also be taken into consideration when determining whether a particular practice is biblical: (1) Is the practice biblically allowable? (2) Is the practice biblically necessary, or an absolute norm—in other words, is it something we must all experience?

The difference between the two is profound. From a biblical perspective, to ask, "*May* I have [or do] this?" is vastly different from the question "*Must* I have [or do] this?" For a manifestation to be biblical, does it also necessarily mean that it is mandatory under all circumstances? And if something is biblically allowable or even commendable, does it mean that it absolute?

In both cases, clearly not. There could be a whole range of biblically allowable experiences and reactions to the presence of God without those same experiences being commanded as necessary for all who experience God's presence. To use one illustration from the Gospels, Jesus healed a blind man using a combination of spit and dirt to create mud to put on the man's eyes. (See John 9:1–7.) Does that mean this is a mandated method of healing? No, Jesus was following the specific leading of the Spirit at that particular time.

Thus, regardless of how powerfully the Holy Spirit may be working in or through physical manifestations, it is a fallacy to say that one *must* experience certain effects (phenomena or manifestations) unless the Bible clearly teaches that is the case.

For example, most classical Pentecostals would argue from Scripture that speaking in tongues is both the definitive sign/gift and the initial evidence that accompanies the baptism of the Holy Spirit. However, it is not possible to argue that recipients of the baptism must also experience all the other biblically allowable phenomena or physical effects (fire, wind, laughter, shaking, and so forth) in order for their experience to be valid.

Neither could we argue that the initial evidence is speaking in tongues alone. Subsequent movements of the Holy Spirit, especially the Third Wave movement, did not limit the scriptural evidence of the baptism of the Holy Spirit to that one manifestation of the Spirit. They cited Acts 19:6, *"And when Paul had laid hands upon them, the Holy Spirit came on them and they began speaking with tongues **and prophesying**."* Rather than focusing primarily on tongues, they emphasized the increase of God's power in the believer's life, as indicated in Acts 1:8. Speaking in tongues became one of the evidences but not the sole and definitive evidence. I think that was a healthy shift in perspective.

Therefore, moving from the question "Must I?" to "Can I"? to "Do I get to?" becomes quite a shift in motivation and obligation. We need to be wary of imposing on people a pressure to perform or to exhibit a particular phenomenon regarding the baptism or other expressions of the Holy Spirit.

Just a brief note in this respect: There may be some places where worshipping in a certain way is appropriate and other places where it may not be—not due to concerns about it being valid or invalid but because we seek peace and unity in the church. It may not be a certain church's custom, and the Holy Spirit may not be working in the same way in that church. I move in the gifts and manifestations of the Holy Spirit in different ways in different settings, as God leads. If I am a visiting speaker at a church, it is not my authority to set the "house rules." The leadership of that church does, under God's direction.

The Holy Spirit has many different ways in which He wants to work, and if we are going to welcome revival, then manifestations and phenomena are part of the package. But we must follow the Spirit's guidance at all times.

ARE THE FRUITS GOOD?

Once it is generally established that a practice or an experience is biblical, it may still not be clear whether a particular experience is actually from God. That is why the Bible puts forward other tests. Ultimately, we must ask the question, regarding any manifestation or phenomenon, "Is there good fruit in relation to it?"

Jesus said the following about false prophets who were to come:

Every good tree bears good fruit, but a bad tree [eventually] *bears bad fruit.... So then, you will know them by their fruits.*
(Matthew 7:17, 20)

Jesus was not directly speaking about spiritual phenomena when He made these statements. However, the principle that Jesus applied to false prophets can also be applied to spiritual experiences. Any experience, even though it may be judged as biblically allowable in itself, must be rejected if it does not pass the test of good fruit.

Jesus made this very point at another time when He stressed that certain miraculous phenomena of prophecy, demon expulsion, and signs and wonders, though biblical in themselves, were actually not from Him because those who practiced them did not have a relationship with Him. (See Matthew 7:21–23.) Surely, Jesus was warning His followers that whether a phenomenon was outwardly a biblical practice could not, by itself, determine whether that spiritual activity was from God. There must be the additional evidence of fruit.

Let us keep in mind that gifts are given, while fruit is grown. God freely gives gifts according to His sovereign will, not because of our good performance but as a demonstration of His great grace. Gifts may be given immediately, while fruit develops through cultivation over a period of time. Therefore, the fruit test often requires observation over various seasons for confirmation.[61]

---

61. For more on this subject and "Nine Scriptural Tests for Revelation," please refer to my books *The Seer*, *The Discerner* (New Kensington, PA: Whitaker House, 2017), and *Hearing God's Voice Today* (Ada, MI: Chosen Books, 2016).

Over the centuries, there have been many accounts of good fruits resulting from experiences with God among very diverse movements. These fruits ranged from physical and emotional healings to restored marriages and many other positive changes in lifestyle. A particularly noticeable good fruit was a deepening spirituality of the heart and soul. People have testified to experiencing a greater love for Christ and a greater desire for the Word, prayer, and Christian community, as well as an increasing readiness to be an effective witness of the gospel.

If a person is firmly persuaded that revival phenomena are not from God, they will discount the evidence of good fruit and opt for another explanation. For example, some people might point out that several new age practices give people peace, some cults appear to restore marriages, and other good results can come from dubious sources. In making these observations, they reject the testimony of the fruit. This type of reasoning is highly selective. It ignores the distinct Christian fruit, such as people's conversions to Christ and deepening relationships with Him.

However, the argument remains valid that if something is proven to be against Scripture, then we are bound to reject it, no matter what the benefits or seeming benefits appear to be. Once more, this question must be settled, based on the guidelines we have just discussed: "Is this experience biblical?"

GOD ENCOUNTERS ARE FOR EVERYONE!

Once, while I was having a conversation with the vice president of God Encounters Ministries (GEM)[62] in my living room, the atmosphere suddenly shifted. In a vision, I saw a cylinder of "God presence" in the form of fire. It was amber in color, filled the room from floor to ceiling (this room had a very high ceiling), and was full of motion. There appeared to be a circular staircase in the midst of it.

---

62. God Encounters Ministries (originally called Ministry to the Nations) began over thirty years ago, started by James and Michal Ann Goll. The vision of GEM is to equip and mobilize the body of Jesus Christ by teaching and imparting the power of intercession, prophetic ministry, and life in the Spirit—carrying the presence of God into all of the cultural spheres of society and life. GEM uses a variety of tools and approaches that reach hundreds of thousands of people each year via books, online webinars and classes, resource materials, conferences, media, podcasts, GEM Missions, mentoring programs, and so much more.

When I walked up to this electric presence of God made manifest, a voice from the Lord spoke to me, "My Word is active and alive." The fear of the Lord increased in the room. I put my hand within the swirling fire, and, once again, I heard, "My Word is alive and active." This happened three times. The room was filled with awe and wonder.

Later, after prayer and meditation, I came to understand that I had encountered a realm of the "God DNA molecule." The Holy Spirit spoke to me that God's DNA is His Word, and *"the word of God is alive and active"* (Hebrews 4:12 NIV). God's Word is full of life. Revival manifestations and phenomena are full of life and lead to the God of life!

If we really want renewal and revival, we will welcome the empowering Holy Spirit, who does not always come gently but often arrives with great potency. Joel 2:28–29 promises,

> *And afterward, I will pour out my Spirit on all people. Your sons and daughters will prophesy, your old men will dream dreams, your young men will see visions. Even on my servants, both men and women, I will pour out my Spirit in those days.* (NIV)

Always remember this: when we line up with the Word and the Spirit, God encounters are for everyone!

LET'S PRAY TOGETHER

Father, in the mighty name of Jesus, we want more of Your amazing presence in our lives, families, and cities. We welcome the manifestations and phenomena of the Holy Spirit's power. We welcome the gifts of the Spirit. We welcome the fire of the Spirit. We welcome the wind of the Spirit. We welcome the moving of the Spirit—and we ask You to move in whatever ways You choose. Help us to avoid the ditches and the excesses that can be associated with revival manifestations. We desire the wisdom and truth that come from the combined revelation of Your Word and Your Spirit. Help us to learn from past outpourings and revivals, while, at the same time, not building monuments to them. We want to bear good spiritual fruit, and we want to bring glory to Your name. Send revival now, for Jesus Christ's sake. Amen and Amen!

11

PROPHETIC PROMISES OF THE GREAT HARVEST

"Lord, I have heard the report about You, and I was afraid. Lord,
revive Your work *in the midst of the years, in the midst of the years*
make it known. In anger remember mercy."
—Habakkuk 3:2

This chapter is based on an incredibly rich prophetic history that I have experienced with many men and women of God. I have had the tremendous honor of hearing prophetic promises directly from those through whom God spoke, in various settings, so this topic is very tender and personal to me. In fact, I feel that I am one of several people appointed to be a bridge from one generation to the next: to connect a culture of honor from the generation that went before us to the current generation, so that we will see the fulfillment of the prophetic promises of the great harvest. Thus, this chapter is the culmination of decades of prayer and seeking God.

Our Scripture theme is the prayer from Habakkuk 3:2:*"Revive Your work in the midst of the years, in the midst of the years make it known"*! This plea is similar to the one we looked at in Psalm 85:6: *"Will You not revive us again, so that Your people may rejoice in You?"* Let us pray together in a similar way as we prepare to explore this inspiring aspect of revival breakthrough:

Father, we hunger and thirst for more—for an increasing measure of Your presence and for an increasing fulfillment of Your promises. We ask that You would move upon our hearts by the Holy Spirit and awaken us to the times in which we live. Let us honor the precious stewardship that we have been given for these days. Revive us, and revive Your work in the world. Thank You in advance for Your insights and revelations for us. For Your holy name's sake, Amen and Amen.

In the previous chapter, we talked about various signs and wonders as manifestations of revival. We will also see signs and wonders in the physical world in relation to revival and the great harvest. Joel 2:31 says, *"The sun will be turned into darkness, and the moon into blood, before the great and awesome day of the LORD comes."* Such signs and wonders are for the purpose of creating a supernatural atmosphere of awe, wonder, and the fear of the Lord so that people will turn to God for salvation and deliverance. *"And it will come about that everyone who calls on the name of the LORD will be saved"* (Joel 2:32).

BIBLICAL PROMISES OF OUTPOURING, REVIVAL, AND GREAT HARVEST

As I have described throughout this book, the great harvest will follow our return to the Lord, repentance, engagement in the sacrifice of fasting, and increased expectation that God will move in our midst. But what can we expect in this coming great harvest?

We begin, as always, with the foundation of revelation from Scripture. There are numerous promises in the Bible concerning the great end-times harvest. While we don't know whether the next harvest will be the final one on the earth, or a prelude to that finale, it will be greater than any we have previously experienced.

The following are some biblical promises related to outpouring, revival, and harvest. We have looked at some of these promises in previous chapters. I encourage you to read each passage and meditate on it in the context of our revival breakthrough focus:

PROMISES OF A GLOBAL OUTPOURING

*For I will pour water on the thirsty land, and streams on the dry ground; **I will pour out my Spirit on your offspring, and my blessing***

on your descendants. *They will spring up like grass in a meadow, like poplar trees by flowing streams.* (Isaiah 44:3–4 NIV)

*And afterwards **I will pour out my Spirit on all people.** Your sons and daughters will prophesy, your old men will dream dreams, your young men will see visions. Even on my servants, both men and women, I will pour out my Spirit in those days. I will show wonders in the heavens on the earth, blood and fire and billow of smoke. The sun will be turned to darkness and the moon to blood before the coming of the great and dreadful day of the LORD. And everyone who calls on the name of the LORD will be saved; for on Mount Zion and in Jerusalem there will be deliverance, as the LORD has said, even among the survivors whom the LORD calls.* (Joel 2:28–32 NIV)

*In the last days, God says, **I will pour out my Spirit on all people.** Your sons and daughters will prophesy, your young men will see visions, your old men will dream dreams. Even on my servants, both men and women, I will pour out my Spirit in those days, and they will prophesy. I will show wonders in the heavens above and signs on the earth below, blood and fire and billows of smoke. The sun will be turned to darkness and the moon to blood before the coming of the great and glorious day of the Lord. And everyone who calls on the name of the Lord will be saved.* (Acts 2:17–21 NIV)

PROMISES OF REVIVAL

*You, Lord, showed favor to your land; you restored the fortunes of Jacob. You forgave the iniquity of your people and covered all their sins. You set aside all your wrath and turned from your fierce anger. **Restore us again, God our Savior,** and put away your displeasure toward us. Will you be angry with us forever? Will you prolong your anger through all generations? Will you not revive us again, that your people may rejoice in you?* (Psalm 85:1–6 NIV)

*Oh, that you would rend the heavens and come down, that the mountains would tremble before you! As when fire sets twigs ablaze and causes water to boil, come down to make your name known to your enemies and cause the nations to quake before you. For when you did awesome things that we did not expect, **you came down, and the mountains trembled before you**. Since ancient times no one has heard, no ear has perceived, no eye has seen any God besides you, who acts on behalf of those who wait for him.* (Isaiah 64:1–4 NIV)

*Come, let us return to the LORD. He has torn us to pieces but he will heal us; he has injured us, but he will bind up our wounds. **After two days he will revive us; on the third day he will restore us** that we may live in his presence. Let us acknowledge the LORD; let us press on to acknowledge him. As surely as the sun rises, he will appear; he will come to us like the winter rains, like the spring rains that water the earth.* (Hosea 6:1–3 NIV)

PROMISES OF THE GREAT HARVEST

*Put in the sickle, **for the harvest is ripe**.* (Joel 3:13)

*I looked, and there before me was a white cloud, and seated on the cloud was one like a son of man with a crown of gold on his head and a sharp sickle in his hand. Then another angel came out of the temple and called in a loud voice to him who was sitting on the cloud, "Take your sickle and reap, because the time to reap has come, for the harvest of the earth is ripe." So he who was seated on the cloud **swung his sickle over the earth and the earth was harvested**. Another angel came out of the temple in heaven, and he too had a sharp sickle. Still another angel, who had charge of the fire, came from the altar and called in a loud voice to him who had the sharp sickle, "Take your sharp sickle and gather the cluster of grapes from the earth's vine, because its grapes are ripe." The angel swung his sickle on the earth, gathered its grapes, and threw them into the great winepress of God's wrath.* (Revelation 14:14–19 NIV)

There are times of sowing, times of watering, and times of reaping. My life has been woven around the harvest verse of Joel 3:13: *"Put in the sickle, for the harvest is ripe."* Preparing believers to participate in the harvest has been an integral part of my spiritual calling. You see, the harvest can be ripe, but we have to do our part to bring it to fruition. If we don't, the harvest might rot in the field. Timing is also crucial to reaping a harvest. That is why Jesus said, *"The harvest is plentiful, but the laborers are few; therefore plead with the Lord of the harvest to send out laborers into His harvest"* (Luke 10:2). If we do not recognize when the harvest is ripe and take action to bring it in, we may completely miss the fruit of the years and even the generations during which many people have sowed into good ground for this harvest.

WAVES OF RENEWAL AND REVIVAL IN RECENT DECADES

How can we sense God working in our day for the fulfillment of His promise of a great harvest? Recent history can help to instruct us. The following are waves of revival that occurred in the 1980s and 90s:

+ The Argentinean Revival

+ The South Korean church explosion and cell-church emphasis

+ The Church Growth Institute: C. Peter Wagner

+ The Third Wave Movement: John Wimber

+ The vision of a world harvest: Reinhard Bonnke and others

+ The birth of the Prophetic Movement: various prophets and seers

+ The Toronto Blessing

+ The Brownsville Revival in Pensacola, Florida

+ The God Chasers movement: Tommy Tenney

+ Many revival hubs that subsequently emerged and are still coming forth

I have had the honor of being involved with almost every one of the abovementioned revivals. I ministered in Argentina with the revival leaders there, and I have even been part of major spiritual gatherings, prophesying the beginnings of various Holy Spirit movements. I prophesied concerning the Toronto Blessing, and I prophesied over Steve Hill before the

Pensacola Revival broke forth. I also helped to identify the anointing on Tommy Tenney. I am blessed to have had these callings and to be able to count them as part of my spiritual journey.

The history of revival reveals various ebbs and flows, including periods preceding revival in which people engage in prayer, receive prophetic revelation, and increase their expectation that God will move. Yet revival history also contains "suddenlies." I use this term to describe when revival comes in unexpected ways, in unexpected places, through unexpected people. Yes, in revival, God will sometimes come quickly to His temple: *"And **the Lord, whom you are seeking, will suddenly come to His temple;** and the messenger of the covenant, in whom you delight, behold, He is coming"* (Malachi 3:1). We must not be asleep but wide awake when the harvest is ready and when the Lord suddenly appears!

After the waves of revival in the 1980s and '90s, there was a shift to apostolic hubs and prophetic centers, and thus the second apostolic age of the church began. As described earlier, we have seen a restoration of the five-fold ministry gifts, creating new wineskins to receive the new wine. We have seen the emergence of houses of prayer and healing rooms. We have seen generations and genders coming together in unity. We have seen the development of training centers, e-church services, and online teaching sessions. And we are now seeing the convergence of the ages, including the passing of the baton. From one generation to the next, the new era begins. As it says in Joshua 4:14, *"On that day the LORD exalted Joshua in the sight of all Israel, so that they revered him, just as they had revered Moses all the days of his life."*

ONE MIGHTY RUSHING RIVER

We stand on the edge of God's revival fire, which is burning around the world in the twenty-first century as church explosion and intense persecution occur at the same time. This is the time of greater glory—and greater cost. Will we remain hungry and desperate, lifting a cry of "More, Lord"? Or will we be worn down by the spirit of this age and allow weariness to take its toll?

Let's arise and see a great and mighty rushing river of God come forth! Let's hold fast to the prophetic words that have been given, remembering that we are stewards of these great promises. We must combine our faith with the promises to see them come to pass, for the glory of King Jesus!

WORDS FROM THREE FATHERS OF THE GLOBAL PROPHETIC MOVEMENT

Not only do we have many biblical prophetic promises about the great harvest, but we also have many revelatory prophetic promises that the Holy Spirit has given in recent decades. Some of the most strategic prophetic declarations released in the last generation came through three diverse prophetic fathers: Paul Cain, Bob Jones, and Bishop Bill Hamon. I am thankful to have had personal relationships with Paul and Bob over the years before their passing, and I continue to have a significant relationship with Bishop Hamon today. The following is a brief overview of their major prophetic revelations, which continue to shape where we are today in the church and where we are headed in the great harvest.

PAUL CAIN (1929-2019)

Paul Cain was originally known as the "boy preacher." In his lifetime, he preached before thousands of people, in many countries, in various movements of the Holy Spirit. As a profoundly gifted seer prophet, Paul was given stewardship of some of the greatest prophetic promises any generation has ever known. The promise of which many of us eagerly await the fulfillment is the prophetic declaration concerning "Stadium Christianity." When this word comes to fulfillment, the media will not have any bad news to proclaim because there will only be good news to announce. Stadiums around the planet will be filled with the proclamation of the gospel of the kingdom, and amazing signs and wonders will take place. Paul prophesied:

> I saw that all of the great stadiums and all of the football fields and auditoriums all over the country were just filled with people seeking God. And it seemed as though in this one place I was allowed to be an observer. There were men like we see here tonight, people like we see just all over this giant platform and they had stretchers, hospital gurneys, and they had cots with bodies on them. People were sick. They had invalids. I tell you, the invalid section wasn't back in some old tent adjacent to the big tent where nobody could see them like in the old days. But they were all out there before the people. All of these people were walking around

and over the loudspeaker came words like this, and I heard it just as clear as I am hearing my voice now and much clearer, "We have a resurrection! We have a resurrection! This man was in the county hospital and he was pronounced dead this morning at 11:00. We have a resurrection! He's come back to life!"

And then you just see people rejoicing and magnifying God and it was just like a heavenly symphony. Everybody was making the most beautiful harmonious worship and then another declaration, "We have another resurrection! This person had been dead, and they just rose from the dead!" And then cripples and paralytics would be healed and step out of wheelchairs and people rather than going wild and giving some, you know, great ovation, their voices would just come up as a great orchestration.

I remember I would just seemingly know that God had a string ensemble. He had a brass section. He had all the full-piece orchestra and the voices of these people and it was a beautiful symphony. It was a beautiful symphony of life, thrilling me to life. And so, as they were worshipping, then that would die down. And then other paralytics would get up and walk and other signs and wonders would occur before the vast multitudes there. And this would be going on all over the world. And then I found myself in front of a television set, and when I turned the dial on, the very first thing I began to hear was a news anchorman saying...and this would be on ABC, CBS and NBC and CNN...all of the major networks, I believe, will carry a story like this one day. Only good news, seemingly. We just have good news tonight. And there are no sporting events to announce because all of the sports fields and all of the coliseums are filled with multitudes of people, and you'll never believe what's happening. Or perhaps you will, but there are resurrections from the dead. Paralytics are walking out of the wheelchairs, dropping special devices, and there's all kinds of healing and miracles. And it seems as though they're falling on their face in these stadiums. They're falling on their face and worshipping God. They're singing all these choruses, and folks, we don't know who these people are. They're almost faceless people.

And I tell you, that is really thrilling because God is going to have a people that will be so much like Jesus that you can't see them for the Presence. And the Presence of God is there. And it seems like the whole world is falling on their face and saying, "Jesus is Lord! Jesus is Lord!" and it's here, there, and everywhere. All stadiums are filled around the world seemingly and the world is turning to God! Listen, friends, the Church is going to become that first line of defense again. You hold that and remember it.[63]

The above is one of the many descriptions from Paul Cain about Stadium Christianity. This prophecy is remarkable. It isn't about one stadium being filled. It is about *stadiums* all over the world being filled. In Joel 2:28 and Acts 2:17, we read, "*I will pour out my Spirit on all people*" (NIV).

BOB JONES (1930-2014)

Bob Jones was one of the most unusually gifted seer prophets of his generation and possibly of any generation. He went before the Lord in a near-death encounter and was sent back with multiple messages directly from Jesus Himself. Bob came back to identify and anoint leaders who would later become fathers and mothers and trainers of leaders who would raise up the harvesters that would see a massive soul harvest, especially of youth. We inherit these great promises to see them come to pass. Here is a prophetic word from Bob:

[The Lord told me], "I'm going to send you back, so that you can go to the leadership of the church that is rising up now and prepare them for a billion souls I'm going to bring to Myself in one of the greatest awakenings of all times." I looked into the face of the Lord and I said, "Lord, I'll go back. I'll go back for just one soul. I'd go back and die on the cross for three days for one soul." And the Lord said, "Bob, I'm sending you back to prepare the people, for I'm going to bring in a billion souls into Myself in one great harvest, and most of them are going to be youth."[64]

---

63. Paul Cain, "I See Stadiums," in Ken Gott, Paul Cain, and Stacey Campbell, *Prayers for the Harvest*, Praying the Bible series, MP3 recording. Used by permission.
64. Bob Jones, "Life Death Encounter," in *Open Heavens* vol. 1 by Wesley and Stacey Campbell, MP3 recording.

It was not that Bob would be the only person who would identify these pivotal spiritual leaders of the new generation, but he was given a commission to identify and empower and help prepare and equip leaders and other believers for a great harvest by speaking words like the one above. After this prophecy was given, there were subsequent signs indicating that we are now at the beginning of the fulfillment of this word. Note that the prophecy talks about "one great harvest," although it does not specifically say "the final harvest." But this is another great prophetic promise that has not yet been fully realized and of which we will be the recipients.

BISHOP BILL HAMON

Bishop Bill Hamon is the founder of Christian International Ministries, a leading prophetic ministry for over forty-five years. A prophet for sixty years, he has prophesied to more than fifty thousand people and provided training for over two hundred fifty thousand in prophetic ministry. Bishop Hamon has possibly been used to activate more people into prophetic gifts than any individual leader in all of church history. He is also a historian of the apostolic and prophetic movements and has written sound doctrinal books that have grounded thousands of believers in these aspects of ministry. The following is an example of the depth of the prophetic gift, combined with a foundational understanding of the apostolic realm, that he demonstrates in his ministry:

> Another restoration truth is coming to the Church that will bring us into full reality.... Twelve Israeli spies went into the land of Canaan. They all saw the same bountifulness and truthfulness of which God had told them about the land. But ten of them were overwhelmed with the giants and walled cities and fortified areas. Joshua and Caleb saw the impossibilities in the natural, but they believed God's promise and said, "We are well able to overcome it" (Num. 13:30). Then ten unbelieving spies said, "We are not able" (Num.13:31)....
>
> This next challenge of the Holy Spirit to the Church of the restoration of the fifth doctrine [the resurrection of the dead] will sound just as unreasonable, irrational, impossible, and ridiculous to the majority of present-day ministers as possessing Canaan did

to the 10 natural-minded Israelites.… The Church will be separated into two groups: the "we are able" group and the "we are not able" group.[65]

As we approach the great harvest, let us be sure to be among the "we are able" group!

PROPHETIC WORDS BY RICK JOYNER, CHUCK PIERCE, CHÉ AHN, JILL AUSTIN, JAMES W. GOLL, AND MIKE BICKLE

We now turn to the words of some additional prophetic voices from contemporary times.

RICK JOYNER: THE MARVEL OF THE AGES

The Lord has prepared a ministry for the last days that will be the marvel of men and angels. These will not be self-seeking or self-promoting, and most of them will remain unknown to the world—even to much of the church. Their works and preaching will stir nations, but many will fade into the crowds and disappear before anyone even knows who they are.

Many of the most powerful apostles and prophets will remain nameless and faceless to the public. These have no desire to build major ministries and will not covet fame or fortune.… Their whole purpose is to see the King's joy because they are truly His friends. These will follow Him wherever He goes.…

Not since Jesus walked the earth has the enemy feared anyone like he does these selfless messengers of power. Just as he tried to destroy Moses and Jesus by killing the children, his present onslaught through abortion, drugs, and disease is a desperate attempt to destroy these before they can mature by destroying their generation.…

In the near future, the church will not be looking back at the first-century church with envy because of the great exploits of those days, but all will be saying that He certainly did save His

65. Bill Hamon, *The Eternal Church* (Shippensburg, PA: Destiny Image Publishers, 2007), 309.

best wine for last. The most glorious time in all of history has now come upon us. You who have dreamed of one day being able to talk with Peter, John, and Paul are going to be surprised to find that they have all been waiting to talk to you! You have been chosen to see the harvest, the fruit of the seeds that they were planting.[66]

God will pour out the great harvest as we humble ourselves before Him and align our wills with His.

CHUCK PIERCE: FROM CHURCH ERA TO KINGDOM ERA

We are moving from a church era to a kingdom era.

In this divine shift the Lord is transforming our mindset, so we move outwardly from what has been built in one season into a new movement for the next season. This will be a new building season, but first we must unlock God's kingdom plan and align heaven and earth....

We must remember it took approximately seventy years to establish the first church era. In every era we unlock a kingdom plan so we can build the prototype for the ecclesia for the future. This new era propels us into a season of unlocking so that we can build in days ahead. That is exactly what God is doing—*right now.*

He is "passing over" His people, looking for His church—that body of believers who will be used in this *pey* [a Hebrew term meaning "voice" or "mouth"] decade of harvest in the midst of world turmoil. While this entire *pey* decade is strategic, there is a seven-year period—late fall of 2019 through 2026—that will be *most critical.* During these seven years we will see great rearrangement of economic power structures as well as spiritual power shifts. Watch. Pray.... And when God releases you in your particular sphere and authority, move forward in boldness, not backward in fear.[67]

This word seems especially timely given the global shaking we have seen in the first three years of this seven-year period. In these days, let

---

66. Rick Joyner, *The Harvest* (Fort Mill, SC: MorningStar Publications, 2011), 23–26.
67. Chuck Pierce, *The Passover Prophecies* (Lake Mary, FL: Charisma House, 2020), chap. 3, Kindle. Italics are in the original.

us remember that we are to move forward in boldness, as the Lord leads, rather than surrender to fear.

CHÉ AHN: A PROPHETIC SEASON OF REVIVAL

I believe that the decade we now find ourselves in, the 2020s, will be a decade of revival. The Church is being called to move forward and cultivate a lifestyle of extraordinary prayer. I believe we are to take action—on our knees in prayer—and lay the foundation for what the Holy Spirit is about to do in our nation [the United States]. We are in the prophetic season of revival.

There is a temptation to lose our fervency in prayer when things seem to be happening sovereignly. On the contrary, we have learned that when God pours out His unmerited grace, we should give ourselves to prayer as never before (see 1 Thessalonians 5:17). Our God is more than able to bring reformation to our land and revival to our hearts. We need to give Him no rest until multitudes are swept into the Kingdom and a radical transformation is seen in all areas of society.

To this end we continue to labor, pray, and believe! In this historic hour, the Lord is moving like never before, so we must press forward until we see the Kingdom of heaven invading our hearts, home, and nation....

...It is time for extraordinary prayer—to prepare for the greatest harvest the world has ever seen![68]

JILL AUSTIN (1948-2009): BRIDAL PARTNERSHIP

Jill Austin was an award-winning potter and the founder of Master Potter Ministries. Before her passing, she was a leading prophetic voice. In her book *Dancing with Destiny*, she shared God's heart for the those whom He desires to gather in His great harvest:

There are so many broken ones whom the Lord wants to heal and save. He wants us to take off our blinders. He wants us to see

---

68. Ché Ahn, *Turning Our Nation Back to God: Through Historic Revival* (Jurapa Valley, CA: Wagner Publications, 2022), chap. 9, Kindle.

those people in our neighborhoods who do not quite measure up to what we would expect to find in church. We need to hear His cry for us to move in bridal partnership. We can be ones who move throughout the harvest to gather the people God has called to be part of the Body.

This is a love message. Rahab is a prophetic picture of the end time Church. The Bride of Christ will be birthed from the most unlikely places. He comes and finds these devastated, hurting, despised, culturally rejected and broken people and tells them He loves them. He says, "I will fill your empty heart. I will clothe you. I will take away your rags. You will no longer be called forsaken and desolate. I call you Beulah. I call you married one."

Do we tend to go only on mission trips to the "poor"? Or do we hear the Lord when we are in board meetings, in coffee shops, in schools or in the computer world? Do we say, "Lord, start to give me divine strategies. I want to hear Your word. I am willing to go into battle. Show me Your plans for the end time harvest"?[69]

JAMES W. GOLL: A YOUTH EXTRAVAGANZA

As described earlier, the great harvest will include masses of young people. In 1995, the Lord was moving upon me with wave upon wave of His Holy Spirit. One night, I had an intense dream and visionary experience in which I saw stadiums filled with young people praising God. This vision aligned with the "Stadium Christianity" that Paul Cain prophesied about.

In the dream, I heard this piercing word: "The stadiums will be filled, as out of the belly of the Promise Keepers movement shall come forth a Youth Extravaganza that will rock the nations." I woke up from the dream only to be catapulted into an open vision and hear myself prophesying these same words with the electric presence of God all over the words and the presence of God saturating my bedroom.

I saw an enormous digital board at one end of a football stadium that was filled with young people worshipping God. The screen depicted the

69. Jill Austin, *Dancing with Destiny: Awaken Your Heart to Dream, to Love, to War* (Ada, MI: Chosen Books, 2007), 127.

crucifixion of Jesus. Lights were crisscrossing the sky until they came into a convergence at the center above the stadium and formed a cross high and lifted up for everyone to see. The spirit of conviction fell upon multitudes, and I heard people crying out, "What must I do to be saved?" The presence of the Lord was being mightily poured out as a new radical Jesus People Movement was being birthed worldwide.

In this regard, let's look at the promises in Psalm 110:1–3:

> The LORD says to my Lord: "Sit at My right hand until I make Your enemies a footstool for Your feet." The LORD will stretch out Your strong scepter from Zion, saying, "Rule in the midst of Your enemies." **Your people will volunteer freely on the day of Your power;** in holy splendor, from the womb of the dawn, **Your youth are to You as the dew.**

I heard this psalm preached on at the height of the Jesus People Movement. One of the reasons I dedicated my life to full-time Christian service was because I had a conviction about the authority of that word: "Your people will volunteer freely in the day of Your power." And that word goes out again now for a Youth Extravaganza—for multitudes of young people to come to the Lord and freely and wholeheartedly serve Him.

MIKE BICKLE: ESTABLISHING THE FIRST COMMANDMENT TO FIRST PLACE

In May 2022, I attended The Send missional gathering in Kansas City, Missouri. At the gathering, Mike Bickle related how, in July 1988, he received a word from the Lord through Bob Jones. That word encapsulates the heart of God for us and for millions who do not yet know Him. Mike expanded on that experience in the following account:

> While in my office at the church, I read a wedding invitation that highlighted Song of Solomon 8:6–7. Suddenly, the Holy Spirit began to move strongly on me to such a degree that I called our church receptionist to ask for privacy. I told her, "Something is happening. Please don't let anybody come to my office during the next hour." About ten minutes later, the phone in my office rang. When I answered the phone, the receptionist said, "Bob Jones is calling you." Bob had an established prophetic ministry in

our midst. When the receptionist connected the call, Bob told me, "Mike, I just heard the audible voice of the Lord. I heard the Lord say, 'Song of Solomon, chapter 8, verses 6 and 7.'"

At that moment, I was kneeling and reading that very passage of Scripture. Then Bob said, "The Lord just told me two things to tell you from Song 8:6–7. First, you are to focus on the spiritual message that is emphasized there all the days of your life—yes, for the rest of your ministry. The spiritual message highlighted there is the first commandment [Matthew 22:37–38]." At that time, in 1988, or almost thirty-five years ago, I'd never thought of focusing on the first commandment for the rest of my ministry. Second, Bob said, "The Lord just told me that He is going to release a great measure of grace on the coming generation to walk in the message set forth in Song 8:6–7."

Then Bob ended his phone call to me. He just hung up. It was about a thirty-second phone call. I didn't say, "Thank you." I didn't say, "Wow." I was awestruck by what Bob had just said, and I wept before the Lord because Bob did not know that, at that very moment, I was on my knees reading Song 8:6–7.

A summary of the spiritual message set forth in Song of Solomon 8:6 is that the Lord would release a seal of fire on the hearts of His people—this is a reference to the first commandment. Walking in the grace or anointing of the first commandment is what will make a believer's life great when they stand before the Lord on the last day. (See 2 Corinthians 5:10.) We do not want to stand before Jesus on that day with regret. I fear regret more than anything. I don't want to stand there, seeing His beautiful face and acknowledging His excellent leadership, and admit with regret that I was half-hearted toward Him. Jesus gave us so much. On that day, we want the testimony that we loved Him in a way that was worthy of who He is.

I believe God is marking this generation with grace to walk in the first commandment. I believe He's going to establish the first commandment in the first place in the body of Christ across the earth before the Lord returns. I prophesy that the Holy Spirit is going to establish the first commandment in the first place in the body of Christ before Jesus returns.[70]

This word from Bob Jones to Mike Bickle emphasized how Song of Solomon 8:6 is a reflection of the first commandment. Let's look at these passages side by side:

Put me like a seal over your heart, like a seal on your arm. For love is as strong as death...its flames are flames of fire, the flame of the LORD.

(Song 8:6)

And [Jesus] said to him, "'You shall love the Lord your God with all your heart, and with all your soul, and with all your mind.' This is the great and foremost commandment." (Matthew 22:37–38)

A great harvest is coming! What is this harvest ultimately about? It is about God's deep love for all those whom He has created. It is about His desire that no one should perish but that everyone should be saved and be restored to a passionate relationship of love and oneness with Him.

May we offer God a love worthy of who He is as we welcome an unprecedented harvest of souls for Him.

LET'S PRAY TOGETHER

Father God, in the majestic name of Jesus, we count it a great honor to be alive in this hour, an hour of prophetic destiny that the prophets of old spoke about. We also consider it an honor that the lamp of the Lord of revelation shines brightly in this day. Holy Spirit, we believe the words of the prophets from times past and of those whom You have sent in more recent times. We add our faith to Your great promise for a billion-soul harvest, especially of youth. We believe a day is coming when stadiums around the world will be filled with people seeking Your face, and signs and wonders will be poured out. Yes, send the promised outpouring of Your Holy Spirit in this very generation, for Jesus Christ's sake! Amen and Amen!

---

70. Used by permission.

12

THY KINGDOM COME! FROM REVIVAL TO AWAKENING AND FROM REFORMATION TO TRANSFORMATION

"Your kingdom come. Your will be done, on earth as it is in heaven."
—Matthew 6:10

This is the final chapter of *Revival Breakthrough*, but it is not the final chapter in your revival journey! I pray that this book has opened a door for you that leads to a corridor with multiple additional doors—dimensions of revival for you to enter as God leads you. In this chapter, we will explore how revival moves into awakening, and how reformation leads to transformation, as the great harvest unfolds and society is transformed.

Our theme Scripture is the familiar but potent declarative pronouncement found in the Lord's Prayer: that God's kingdom would come and that His will would be done on earth as it is in heaven. That is what revival breakthrough is all about! Let us pray that the accumulation of all the Scriptures and prayers and principles and examples and wisdom God has provided for us concerning seasons of glory, awakening, and great harvest will bear fruit in our lives even now:

Father, thank You for leading us this far and for continuing to lead us through this last chapter and beyond so that we will take action steps to help bring revival breakthrough. Inspire and motivate us to seek You behind every door You open for us to enter in this ongoing revival journey. In the name of Your precious Son, Amen and Amen.

THE MODEL PRAYER OF JESUS: HEAVEN'S RULE AND REIGN ON EARTH

The Lord's Prayer is probably one of two most-prayed prayers—if not *the* most-prayed prayer—in all of history. The other may be this prayer, which God gave Moses for blessing His people: "*The LORD bless you, and keep you; the LORD cause His face to shine on you, and be gracious to you; the LORD lift up His face to you, and give you peace*" (Numbers 6:24–26).

I memorized the Lord's Prayer as a child, and you may have done so, as well. I recited it every Sunday with the rest of the congregation at our church. Most liturgical churches, whether Catholic, Orthodox, Anglican, or other mainline Protestant denominations, pray this prayer every week. Let's read the version from the book of Matthew:

Our Father, who is in heaven, hallowed be Your name. Your kingdom come. Your will be done, on earth as it is in heaven. Give us this day our daily bread. And forgive us our debts, as we also have forgiven our debtors. And do not lead us into temptation, but deliver us from evil.
(Matthew 6:9–13)

Although we refer to this passage of Scripture as "the Lord's Prayer," in reality, the term "the Lord's prayer" would better fit the recorded prayer of the Lord Jesus found in John 17. In that prayer, He earnestly prays for His disciples—both His immediate circle of disciples and all the other disciples who would follow Him throughout history, including us today. As we discussed in chapter 3, the prayer from Matthew would be better titled "the Model Prayer" or, even more accurately, "the Disciples' Prayer."

Remember that the disciples had requested that Jesus teach them how to pray, just as John the Baptist was teaching his disciples how to pray. In this passage, the Lord is teaching the disciples how to pray effectively and what basic elements to include in prayer. Again, Jesus didn't give us a line-by-line, rote way to pray but rather prayer *themes*.

Significantly, Jesus did not teach the disciples escapism ("Lord, get us out of here as soon as possible!") but rather how to call forth the rule and reign of heaven *on earth now*. It is essential for us to grasp this truth! It is also good to note that this is not as much a petition form of prayer as it is an imperative form of prayer with more of a command orientation. Thus, it is actually more like, "Kingdom, come! Father's will, be done, on earth as it is done in heaven!"

When we pray for heaven's rule and reign to come to earth, we need to seriously consider the following questions—studying the Scriptures, seeking the Lord, and searching our own hearts for the answers:

+ What is the atmosphere of heaven?

+ What occurs in heaven?

+ What would heaven on earth look like?

+ When are our prayers for God's kingdom to come on earth to transpire?

+ Do we honestly take time to meditate on what we actually believe when we pray?

These are foundational questions whose answers shape our theology.

One time, many years ago, when I was a young pastor, God suddenly showed up and whispered to me, "Your world end-time view will determine your lifestyle." I will never forget that word. The Holy Spirit arrested me that day with a thought that was not my own; it was not something I would normally think about. I was part of the Jesus People movement at the time, and we believed that the return of Jesus was imminent, like *tomorrow*.

I am now seventy years old, and I wish I would have asked God for more understanding of what He meant when He said, "Your world end-time view will determine your lifestyle." I wish I had grasped even 10 percent of what the Lord was trying to talk to me about. Nevertheless, that word went inside me, and that word is still inside me. And now I ask you, knowing that your world end-time view will determine your decisions, are you here on earth merely on your way out to a better place, or are you here to *bring God in*?

As we collaborate with our heavenly Father for His kingdom to come on earth as it is in heaven, we also need to understand what it looks like to go from revival to awakening and from reformation to transformation. We must learn to catch, survive, and thrive with every wave that crashes upon the shores of church history. In this way, we will go *"from glory to glory"* (2 Corinthians 3:18) until Jesus's model prayer is answered!

FROM REVIVAL TO AWAKENING

From my perspective, gained from years of study, prayer, and contemplation, as well as from picking the brains and hearts of many church leaders over the years, I see some overlapping principles between revivals and awakenings, as well as some distinct differences between them. Let's briefly look at their main features.

FEATURES OF REVIVALS

1. Revivals return the church to its first love relationship with God.

2. They are works that restore the church to its place, fervency, impact, and influence.

3. They are often short-lived in duration and therefore emerge in cycles.

4. Many revivals end prematurely because those who are involved often lack a practical theology to guide them in what happens during revival and what is meant to follow after revival.

As we transition to the features of awakenings, let us recognize that every awakening begins with revival. While a revival typically lasts from weeks to several years, an awakening lasts from about ten years to five or six decades.

FEATURES OF AWAKENINGS

1. Awakenings begin with the authentic fire of God reviving people.

2. They empower the renewed believers into societal transformation.

3. Historically, they are longer in length than revivals because the revivalists, who now become reformers, impact and change injustices in multiple realms of society.

4. They are sustained by waves of God's renewing presence, with the participants having a long-term view of a kingdom mandate.

Keeping these features and differences in mind, let us review historical Great Awakenings that have occurred in the past three hundred years.

THE GREAT AWAKENINGS

In the 1700s and 1800s, several Great Awakenings impacted the British Isles and America. Revival historians differ in their assessments of how many awakenings there actually were. Some people think we are still waiting for a third awakening, while others are of the opinion that there may have been more than three. It's not my purpose here to debate that question. Rather, I want to express that *we have experienced genuine widespread awakenings from God in the past*, and we can look to Him to bring about a sustained, transformational work of the Holy Spirit in His church and in our nations once again.

The awakenings in the eighteenth and nineteenth centuries came about during periods when many people's faith had waned and new generations were not being brought up to love and serve the Lord. Under such spiritual leaders as George Whitefield, John Wesley, Jonathan Edwards, Gilbert Tennent, Timothy Dwight, and Charles Finney, people were called to renew their passion for God or to come to faith in Christ for the first time. Masses of people were converted. In these awakenings, there was an emphasis on the new birth, the assurance of salvation, and a personal relationship with Jesus. Throughout church history, much of the church had not understood that one could receive the assurance of salvation, so this was quite a radical change in people's spiritual perspective that was brought about by awakening.

The awakenings also stimulated social transformation. The following are some examples of the many outcomes of these awakenings: There was an increased emphasis on the importance of biblical literacy and training. Renowned Christian colleges, seminaries, and missionary societies were birthed. Benevolence ministries were launched. Humanitarian endeavors, including abolition, gained momentum. Leading Christian organizations, such as the Salvation Army, the YMCA, the Student Volunteer Movement for Foreign Missions, and the Cambridge Inter-Collegiate Christian Union (forerunner to campus ministries such as InterVarsity Christian Fellowship, Cru, and the Navigators), came into being.

To give one illustration of the mass impact of awakening, here is an account of the revivals under Charles Finney:

> By 1832 Finney's revival movement had added several hundred thousand to the churches. His campaign in Rochester, New York, in 1842 seemed to prepare the way for the extensive revival of 1843–44. And his revival campaign in Rochester in 1856 prepared the way of the Lord for the mighty movement of revival that swept America in 1857–58. The people who were led to Christ directly or indirectly by Finney through his personal campaigns, writings, encouragements, and prayer probably brought a million people or more into the kingdom of God. While it is said that 70 percent of the converts even in [D. L.] Moody's meetings became backsliders, it is estimated that 85 percent of the professed converts in the Finney revivals remained true to the Lord.[71]

Previously, I have emphasized how Charles Finney was "possessed by God," having experienced the infilling of the Holy Spirit as "liquid love." When we surrender to the Lord, allowing Him to fill us and use us as individuals, and when we come together with other believers to seek God, pray, and fast, what might God do through us?[72]

FROM REFORMATION TO TRANSFORMATION

Before these Great Awakenings, there was the Great Reformation, without which we probably would not have had these awakenings. This is where awakening and reformation overlap.

There have been various "tipping points" in history that have carried societies and the world at large into significant change. On October 31, 1517, Martin Luther nailed his famous 99 Theses to the door of a church in Wittenberg, Germany. This event became known as the beginning of the Great Reformation. Many forerunners served God's purposes before Martin Luther, but his bold statements of faith propelled great change and created a chain reaction of convulsive transition.

---

71. Duewel, *Revival Fire*, chap. 12, Kindle.
72. To read more about specific revivals and their outcomes, as well as their relationship to prayer, please see my book *Prayer Storm*, chapter 8, "Prayer for Revival in the Church," and chapter 9, "Prayer for Another Great Awakening—Youth."

Luther's primary progressive revelation was based on a rhema, revelatory word from Romans 1:17: *"The just shall live by faith"* (KJV, NKJV). This emphasis on a seemingly overlooked biblical truth renewed a core understanding of the gospel of the Lord Jesus Christ. Instead of being based on human works, it was based on faith in the completed work of the cross of the *"one man, Jesus Christ"* (Romans 5:17 NIV).

We have now lived in the wake of the Great Reformation for the past five hundred years. Many additional lost truths, all based on the Word of God, have since been illuminated and restored to the church in successive waves. These include believer's baptism, the baptism in the Holy Spirit, direct access to the throne of God through Christ, the experience of the presence of God on a daily basis, the empowering of the gifts of the Spirit in and through every believer, the present activity of the fivefold office gifts of the Spirit, including the ministries of apostles and prophets—and so much more! We are now living in the period referred to in Acts 3:21 as *"the period of restoration of all things"*:

> Therefore **repent and return**, so that your sins may be wiped away, in order that times of **refreshing may come from the presence of the Lord**; and **that He may send Jesus**, the Christ appointed for you, whom heaven must receive until **the period of restoration of all things**, about which God spoke by the mouths of His holy prophets from ancient times. (Acts 3:19–21)

This passage states that Jesus Christ will remain in heaven until this period of the restoration of all things spoken of by the prophets of old fully occurs. Only then will He return. Yes, this is an expansive subject, indeed. But what a glorious day it will be when Jesus parts the skies and returns just as He left!

TIME FOR THE GREAT TRANSFORMATION!

So, where do we go from here? In the Bible, fifty is the number of Jubilee. (See, for example, Leviticus 25:8–13.) Five hundred is ten Jubilees! We have crossed the threshold of five hundred years since the Great Reformation. Many prophets have declared that we have entered into a "New Era." Could it be that we are now transitioning from the Great Reformation into the Great Transformation? Are we not transitioning from the church age to the kingdom age, as we talked about in the previous chapter?

You may not have given much thought to your world end-time view. How much have you actually thought about revival breakthrough for your life, for the lives of your family members, for your sphere of influence, and for your city? What are you believing for? Are you living your life moment by moment, or are you building your life for a lineage and a legacy? It's time for a Great Transformation.

THE COMING GLORY OF THE LORD

This brings us full circle to the vision of glory that I received from the Lord, which I related in the preface to this book. The vision occurred one evening in September 2020 when I was going to sleep. I had asked the Lord if He had a dream in His heart and, if so, if He would like to share His dream with me and also give me permission to share His dream with others. I fell right asleep and went into a dream state in which I saw myself sitting up in my bed with my Bible open. I could hear myself reading from Isaiah 60:1–3:

> Arise, shine; for your light has come, and the glory of the LORD has risen upon you. For behold, darkness will cover the earth and deep darkness the peoples; but the LORD will arise upon you and His glory will appear upon you. Nations will come to your light, and kings to the brightness of your rising.

When I woke up from the dream, I was actually sitting up in bed, prophesying from this passage in Isaiah and also Habakkuk 2:14, saying, "Arise, shine, for the glory of the Lord is risen upon you. And the knowledge of the glory of the Lord is going to cover the earth as the waters cover the seas."

Revival Breakthrough is all about God's dream that His glory cover the earth. Again, this move that we are now entering is a "latter glory of God" dream. Let us always remember that the Lord invites us to partner with Him in this dream! But to do this, we need to continually renew our minds to His ways and His will.

In her book *Reformers Arise*, my dear friend Cindy Jacobs challenges us with a prophetic word that the Lord challenged her with. It touches on some important points we discussed in chapter 10 about how our attitudes toward revival manifestations and phenomena are influenced by our mindsets and preconceptions:

Ironically, most of us do not even know that our thinking and worldview have been polluted, or at least influenced, by secularism, naturalism, and humanistic rationalism through our educational system, media, and culture. We do not have a clue as to where to start in the process or reforming our nations.... Even when we come to Scripture, we too often interpret it through culture-tinted glasses rather than digging into God's Word and letting it reform our hearts and renew our thinking....

...God is going to show us how, as a Holy Nation, to begin to affect our world on a reformational level that will produce lasting transformation.... The process of becoming a Holy Nation first requires some major restructuring of our thinking.

This leads to a major point that I want to make:

Our minds need to be discipled
before we can disciple a nation....

...To do that, ask the Holy Spirit to expose to you any way that you have been affected by secularism or any other "ism" that is ungodly.[73]

Cindy goes on to encourage us to pray the following prayer with her.

O Lord,

I need your help! I submit my whole self to You. Please, by the power of the Holy Spirit, come as a divine surgeon into my thinking. Father, anywhere that I have been taught or come to believe what is false thinking—not thinking according to your Word and will for my life—change me. Change the way I think. Renew my mind. I do not want to be conformed to the world but desire to see Your kingdom come and Your will be done on earth as it is in heaven.

In Jesus' name,

Amen.[74]

I encourage you to mediate on this prayer and pray it from your heart.

---

73. Cindy Jacobs, *Reformers Arise: Your Prophetic Strategy for Bringing Heaven to Earth* (Shippensburg, PA: Destiny Image, 2021), 82–85.
74. Jacobs, *Reformers Arise*, 86.

THE GENTLE, THE RUDE, AND THE GREAT AWAKENING

Over the years, I have prophetically spoken about how the coming Great Awakening will take shape. In the early 1990s, the Holy Spirit whispered to me that He would arrive like a gentle rain, but that some people would resist the soaking rain of His presence. Their reaction would expose how humans too often like to control things and not yield to the ways in which God is working. The Holy Spirit referred to this first invitation as the "Gentle Awakening."

But God would not take no as an answer from those who were asleep or did not yield to Him. The Holy Spirit spoke to me, "I will shake My people to wake My people up!" He would come with shaking, more shaking, and even more shaking to awaken us. Many people would be brought to a crossroads: they would either decide to wake up through circumstantial shaking or choose to be offended by this seemingly "Rude Awakening" of the Holy Spirit.

Ultimately, all of these various stages, forms, and waves—the gentle and the "rude"—will work together to create and form the next awakening. God has decided He is coming to shake us awake and prepare us for the greatest awakening the world has ever known.[75]

IT'S TIME TO MAKE A WAVE!

The Lord once gave me a spiritual dream in which I was told, "Don't just wait for the next wave to watch it and possibly catch it. It's time for you to *make* a wave! Don't just wait for the stirring of the waters. You can draw forth the finger of God by the depth of your hunger and create the next wave."

For years, I have sought to encourage and challenge people with this thought: "The depth of your hunger is the length of your reach to God." In partnership with God, it's time to make the next wave!

Let's be among those who believe that we are called to go from glory to glory and that we are invited to be a part of the "Greater Works Generation"—renewed, revived, and reformed—to bring the

75. For more on this subject, see my books *The Coming Israel Awakening* (Ada, MI: Chosen Books, 2009) and *The Mystery of Israel and the Middle East* (Ada, MI: Chosen Books, 2021).

transformation that Jesus prophesied would come: on earth as it is in heaven. Let us volunteer freely in the day of His power!

Stacey Campbell, a friend of many years, is a prophet, a leader, a forerunner, the leader of Global Shiloh, and the author of *Ecstatic Prophecy*.[76] Stacey shared a very special word with me that has deeply touched my heart. It went something like this: "For years, Jesus has given Himself to answering my prayers for my life and family and ministry. But I have come to a place in my life and ministry where I want to live the rest of my days as an answer to the prayers of Jesus. What are You praying, Jesus? What is burning on Your heart, Jesus? I want to pray Your prayers, and I want to commit my life to seeing Your prayers being answered on earth."

Stacey has told me she believes that we are shifting into a time when we will see the model prayer of Jesus answered. Let it be so! This is all part of *Revival Breakthrough* and preparing for an unprecedented harvest of a billion souls and beyond, where the glory of the Lord will cover the earth as the waters cover the seas.

REVIVAL IS GOD'S WORK

May we dedicate ourselves to being the answers to the prayers of Jesus as His model prayer is fulfilled in our world. In my book *Prayer Storm*, I talk extensively about how we can manifest our hunger for God and for revival through our prayers. Here are some excerpts that especially relate to the themes we have discussed in this chapter and throughout this book:

> Prayer is a key ingredient prior to revival, and prayer continues as a key ingredient for sustaining the results of revival....
>
> Prayer, and more prayer, is the appropriate response to desperate times. Extreme prayer at all hours of the day and night is the only appropriate application of effort before, during, and after a time of revival from God. God wants to revive His people, wherever they may live. In other words, revival is *His* work, and the way we participate is to engage *Him* in all prayerfulness....

---

76. Stacey Campbell, *Ecstatic Prophecy* (Ada, MI: Chosen Books, 2008).

Not just any kind of prayer will do. This kind of praying makes you sweat. It is hard work. It's often compared to the travail of childbirth....

Prayer for revival...is prayer for the Kingdom of God to come *here* and *now.* The only effective prayer is that which is inspired by the Holy Spirit, and that prayer, by definition, is going to be "violent," passionate, and untiringly persistent.[77]

In *Prayer Storm,* I also discuss the meaning of this passage from Luke 18 and its implications for revival breakthrough:

And will not God bring about justice for his chosen ones, who cry out to him day and night? Will he keep putting them off? I tell you, he will see that they get justice, and quickly. However, when the Son of Man comes, will he find faith on the earth? (Luke 18:7–8 NIV)

This passage portrays night-and-day prayer. But, you may wonder, why are we convinced that this is what's called for and that it is going to be effective? I have assembled the following list of reasons:

+ 24/7 worship and prayer is what is done in Heaven. Let it therefore be done on earth!

+ 24/7 worship and prayer releases God's justice on the earth.

+ 24/7 worship and prayer fuels the Great Commission (see Matt. 28:19).

+ 24/7 worship and prayer hinders the work of the devil.

+ 24/7 worship and prayer releases revival breakthrough.

+ 24/8 worship and prayer prepares the way for Christ's second coming.[78]

Such an endeavor will take dedicated efforts in which we network with other believers to offer unceasing intercession to God to bring us *revival, awakening, reformation,* and *transformation.*

---

77. James Goll, *Prayer Storm: The Hour That Changes the World* (Shippensburg, PA: Destiny Image, 2013), 187–89, Kindle edition.
78. Goll, *Prayer Storm,* 201.

SEEING A GREAT LIGHT!

To bring our journey together to a conclusion, I must give you one last passage from God's Word:

> *The people who walk in darkness will see a great light; those who live in a dark land, the light will shine on them. You will multiply the nation, You will increase their joy; they will rejoice in Your presence as with the joy of harvest.* (Isaiah 9:2–3)

I bless you and declare that these are the joyful days of the harvest. Put your hand to the sickle, for the harvest is ripe. Rejoice in His presence. Your revival breakthrough has come upon you!

I pray that you will continue strong on your revival journey, building on all that you have learned in this book about creating an opening for God to intervene, engaging in earnest prayer and sacrificial fasting, experiencing the power in God's presence, and living in expectation of the great harvest. Let the cry arise from glory to glory!

LET'S PRAY TOGETHER

Almighty God, we magnify Your great name! You alone are worthy. We want the Lamb of God to receive the rewards of His sufferings. We want to see the great end-times harvest come in, for Jesus Christ's sake. We want to see the body of Christ walking in purity and power. We declare, "Your kingdom come, Your will be done, on earth as it is currently being done in heaven." We are not satisfied with only the next revival wave hitting the church. We want to see a sustained move of God that takes us into societal change in which we go from glory to glory. Raise up reformers for us today as You have done in days past. Raise up another Great Awakening! Take us from the Great Reformation into the New Era of the Great Transformation, for Jesus Christ's sake. Fulfill the dream that is in Your heart. Let Your glory cover the earth as the waters cover the seas. In the mighty name of Jesus, Amen and Amen!

ABOUT THE AUTHOR

James W. Goll is the founder of God Encounters Ministries and the Kindred Heart Society. He is an international best-selling author, a certified Life Language Coach, an adviser to leaders and ministries, a member of ASCAP, and a vocal recording artist. He is also the founder of Worship City Alliance and Global Prayer Storm, and the cofounder of Compassion Acts and Women on the Frontlines. James is a member of the Harvest International Ministries International Apostolic Team and the Apostolic Council of Prophetic Elders. He serves as an instructor in the Wagner University and the Christian Leadership University. James is also the founder of GOLL Ideation LLC, where creativity, consulting, and leadership training come together.

After pastoring in the Midwest United States, James was thrust into the role of an international equipper and trainer. He has traveled to over fifty nations, sharing the love of Jesus and imparting the power of intercession, prophetic ministry, and life in the Spirit. His desire is to see the body of Christ become the house of prayer for all nations and to see Jesus Christ receive the rewards of His sufferings.

James has recorded numerous classes with corresponding curriculum kits, and he also offers a yearlong mentoring program available globally at mentoringwithjames.com. He is the author of more than fifty books, including *The Seer, The Feeler, The Discerner, Releasing Spiritual Gifts Today,*

Dream Language, Praying with God's Heart, and *The Mystery of Israel and the Middle East.*

James was married to Michal Ann for thirty-two years before her graduation to heaven in the fall of 2008. He has four married children and a growing number of grandchildren. He makes his home in Franklin, Tennessee.

For More Information:

James W. Goll

God Encounters Ministries

P.O. Box 1653

Franklin, TN 37065

Phone: 1-877-200-1604

Websites:

godencounters.com

mentoringwithjames.com/GEM

globalprayerstorm.com

GOLLIdeation.com

E-mails:

info@godencounters.com

linktr.ee/GodEncounters

admin@GollIdeation.com

Social Media:

Facebook, Instagram, YouTube, Vimeo, GEM Media, XP Media, Kingdom Flame, Charisma blogs, iTunes podcasts